# A DRAGON for a Friend

# A DRAGON for a Friend

Anne Conway

A TERRAPIN BOOK

HAMBLESIDE PUBLISHERS LTD.
12, Southgate Street, Winchester, Hampshire.

ISBN 0 86042 022 1

Filmset by Trident Graphics Limited
Printed by Billing & Sons Ltd.

# Part One

# Mr. Nogard

It was the children, chiefly, who looked forward to seeing Mr. Nogard. They were not put off by his long black coat – they never expected him to appear in anything else, and would not have recognised him if he had. All through the winter, busy with school work, sledges, snowfights and all the odd jobs their parents invented when they found them sitting cosy by the fire, they never gave a thought to the man from the hills. But the minute the first blades of daffodil appeared, and fathers began to stamp about in the yard, collecting their tools, and mothers suddenly found corners to clean that no one ever knew existed, then the children would wander up to the village, past the church, past the last house, singing, laughing, tripping each other up, and rolling over and over in the springy turf.

They were not exactly looking for Mr. Nogard, but they knew, as sure as summer sun and birds' nests, that they would find him. He was part of summer, like flying kites or sailing little boats made of rushes, or lying by the stream letting the cold water sparkle over your toes while the sun warmed your face and arms and you dreamed stories into the drifting clouds.

He was often in the village, but no one knew where he lived. He had spoken to every single inhabitant, but no one ever knew him as anything but 'Mr. Nogard'. Everyone else in the village had two or three names. Scrag, or Old Wheezy, was really Jeremiah-by-the-Church. Paula Deluby had once spent the night chasing her precious hen through the hills, and had been called Miss Leghorn ever since, except once, when she had had a letter about some money an aunt had left her. As for Pattyfoot Perkins, at fourteen stone and five foot ten, she was a far cry from the toddler who had pattered down the aisle and said "I will" when Tom and Nora from the mill were being married.

Everyone agreed that there was something strange about Mr. Nogard.

"Where does he come from, I'd like to know," Pattyfoot would say.

"Gives me the creeps, all in black like that. Like a walking shadow," Miss Leghorn would shudder expressively. She was a spinster and lived alone on the other side of the church.

"What's his name anyway – Nogard? Nogood, if

you ask me. Why doesn't he do an honest bit of work instead of hanging around all day, talking to the children. . . ."

All the same, whenever there was any kind of emergency it was extraordinary how the people relied on him. The time Jacob Dooley's tiles blew off in a howling gale, it was Mr. Nogard who travelled twelve miles to the nearest town and brought new ones back so quickly that everyone was afraid to ask how he managed it.

"'Twas almost supernatural speed," said Barney the Tanner as he retold the story for the hundred and sixth time over a pint at Dooley's. And Elsie MacPherson would never forget the day he held her dying baby in his arms. The child was perishing with cold though it was midsummer, and Elsie had tried everything human invention could devise to warm the child. At last in despair she sent for Mr. Nogard. He said nothing when he came, just took the baby and walked round the room. Once or twice he put his lips to the baby's mouth and, Elsie said, "It was as if he was breathing life into my baby again."

Most of the time, though, he was with the children, and to them it never occurred that Mr. Nogard was in any way strange. They realised that he was different from the other grown-ups, but he gave bright silver coins to the bigger ones and lollipops to the little ones, and he was always ready to walk and talk, and make bows and arrows, or play Cowboys and Indians. He was good for making camp-fires, too; he seemed to have a funny knack of licking his fingers, then snapping them to make a spark, and in no time the dry leaves and twigs would be alight. Sometimes his pockets would be bulging, and then the girls would look innocent and say, "I'd love a toasted crumpet" and the boys would dive for his pockets and drag out paper bags stuffed full of fresh, mouthwatering crumpets, enough for one each and a few over. Strangely enough, when the toasting was done, there was never any quarrelling about the extras. Usually a few tasted rather ashy, as crumpets tend to drop into the fire unless your toasting stick is well-shaped or you are an expert of long practice. So the people who got ashy crumpets to start with got the extra ones, and everyone agreed that was fair.

The mothers never worried about their children in the summer. They knew that Mr. Nogard was watching all the time he appeared to be playing with them, and so they were safe. In their hearts they didn't mean all they said about him – they just said it for the sake of gossip, and as no one listened to what anyone else said anyway, none of it really mattered.

# Paul

Paul was different from the other children in some respects. He enjoyed a fight with the best of them and sometimes came home with a bloody nose.

"Haven't I told you not to fight?" his mother would cry, and add a few more bruises to the one he had received in honourable combat. But he might quite suddenly leave the others and wander off, barefoot, across a newly ploughed field, to feel the soft warm earth between his toes and smell its freshness. He noticed things the others took for granted, like the delicate interlocking of a dove's wing feathers. And sometimes he would stand stock still gazing at the drooping beauty of wild fuchsia, or the morning mist as it hung softly over the bay.

The other children often brought presents for Mr. Nogard. Skippy always had sweets, and though she was reluctant to share them with the others, Mr. Nogard was always given one. Spike gave him a set of marbles and a trick frog that jumped at you. Lisa's jacks were on permanent loan to him, and he became, in time, an expert at the game. They gave him things because they liked him and wanted him to like them, and as they clambered round him all talking at the same time about different things, miraculously Mr. Nogard seemed to hear them all and be able to answer them all.

But out of the corner of his eye he was often watching Paul. Paul didn't seem to want to shout with the others, or to hang out of Mr. Nogard's coat tails, or stand on his head in front of him, or ride a bicycle no-hands down the hillside. He could do these things if he felt like it, and he didn't mind if no one was looking; he did them for the sheer fun of it, not for show. Sometimes he even walked away while Mr. Nogard was telling a story – a thing no one else would have done for fear of missing something.

He did sometimes bring things to Mr. Nogard, though; not presents – just things to look at. Once he rescued from the dustbin a single leaf out of a very old book, with gilt edges and ornate lettering. There was an intricate pattern of strange creatures, brightly coloured, winding through leaves and branches of tarnished gold. They looked at it together, and Mr. Nogard read what he could of the strange language in faded ink. For a while they forgot the mountain and the sea, and lived with the ladies of long ago, following them through enchanted forests where good and evil took strange and magic forms. Another day they spent the whole afternoon carving twisted branches, and Paul showed his friend how, if you fitted them together in a certain way, you could make a splendidly antlered deer, or a unicorn. When the sun began to sink and they stood up to go home, they left their two animals guarding the place where they had worked together – a proud, handsome deer made by the craftsman, Paul, and a rather wobbly unicorn put together by the apprentice, Mr. Nogard.

Without realising it Paul was always thinking about Mr. Nogard. If he found a secret cove for fishing he would say, "I'll bring him here – we can catch some good fish together." When he saw rare shells or beautiful stones he would pick them up and put them in his pocket to show him the next day, instead of throwing them back into the sea as he once would have done.

One day Paul had a surprise prepared and he had to wait all day to get Mr. Nogard alone. It seemed as if the other children would never go away. They raced and spun cartwheels and chased each other, until finally, exhausted, they collasped on the grass and demanded a story. As the story unfolded Paul fidgeted. The shadows were lengthening and soon all the others would go home, but so, too, would Mr. Nogard. Paul had never known him to stay after sunset. He tried to concentrate on the story; suddenly the voice stopped and heads looked up in surprise. “Is that the end?” They all had the same feeling that they had missed the middle and woken up as you do in church with a half-guilty start, to hear the priest saying, “Go in peace. Amen.”

“Yes, that’s the end,” said Mr. Nogard, smiling at Paul over the heads of his companions. “Home now, quick, or you’ll be late for tea and then you won’t get out tomorrow.”

There was no arguing and they raced off, hooting and yelling down the stony path to the village, and all were soon out of sight. Only Paul waited.

“Would you like to come and see my den?” he asked shyly. There was a fractional hesitation as Mr. Nogard looked at the setting sun.

“Will you take me?” he replied, and the two walked down the hillside, the man’s hand resting on the boy’s shoulder.

What Paul had in the den would appear quite uninteresting to a stranger. A piece of old root, some broken coloured glass, chippings of wood and stone, paper, boxes, parts of an old bicycle – the kind of thing that any self-respecting mother would have turned out and burned or buried if she had the chance.

But this was not what Mr. Nogard saw. What looked like an old root had become a pipe that played three notes if you knew how to blow it. The bicycle wheels were suspended horizontally from the central rafters, and from the rim dangled pieces of a rabbit’s skeleton that grinned and gyrated in the dim light as the draught from the door caught them.

Mysteries! The little hut was vibrant with the laughter of Mr. Nogard as Paul showed him one after another of his treasures. They tried to play a duet; Paul playing the melody on the root pipe and Mr. Nogard filling in the bass with a wheezy piece of grass. That ended in gales of laughter that carried out into the twilight and surprised even the sparrows into silence. Then, as the laughter subsided and the two friends paused for a breath, a lone thrush trilled a new rich melody across the evening stillness. It was as if she had spent her life learning to sing only for this moment. The den, the treasures, ceased to exist; for an instant the two friends were swept into the soaring melody, and there was only the silvery voice of the bird cascading in the velvet dusk.

As he climbed the path towards the forest Mr. Nogard smiled. "At last," he murmured. Then he turned his face up to the sky. A star was winking brilliantly and he laughed aloud. "At last!" he shouted waving up to the star, and bounded up the path leaping from stone to stone. Now he was at the edge of the forest; he stopped in front of an old, knotted and gnarled tree. It seemed to be grinning at him in the fading light – yes, definitely, the branches were rustling with whispered laughter and the tree was grinning broadly. Mr. Nogard slapped its trunk exuberantly. "It's happened, oak," he cried joyously. "It's happened at last!"

With a leap he bounded into the forest and vanished in the darkness.

The crescent moon smiled radiantly over the valley.

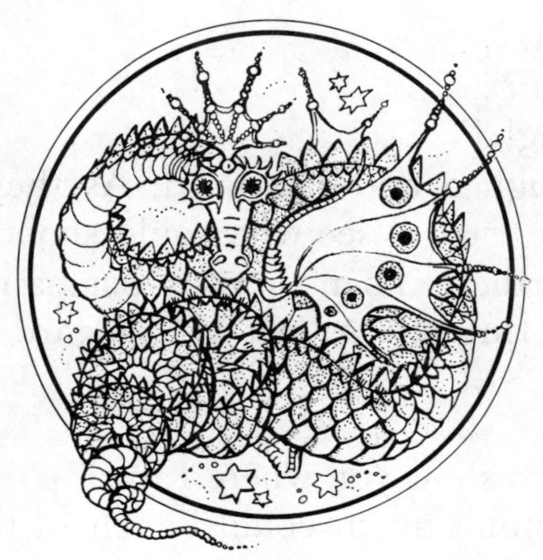

# A Dragon

The next day began with a rolling mist; the farmers looked up to the hills and said, "It'll be a rare scorcher today."

Naturally they were right. By ten o'clock it was pleasantly warm. By noon everyone had gone indoors to make cool drinks and find a little shade. Soon it would be time for the second crop of hay, but not just yet. For today the farmers laid down their tools and unharnessed their horses; everyone had a right to rest in such heat.

So Mr. Nogard was surprised and delighted to find Paul walking towards him as he emerged from the forest.

"Where's everyone else?"

"Indoors."

"On a day like this?"

“Too hot.”

“And you?”

“I’m tough.”

They laughed and sat down. As they lazily ate plums they tried to see who could shoot his plumstone the farthest. Then they lay back and looked at the shimmering sky. At last Mr. Nogard spoke.

“Paul.”

“Mm?”

“I want to show you where I live.”

Paul’s astonishment could be felt in the absolute silence that followed.

“Today?” he asked.

“Now,” said Mr. Nogard. “That is, if you’d like to come.”

Paul sat up. “I didn’t think you had a home,” he gasped.

“Just you wait and see!” shouted the other as they both leapt to their feet. As they walked, the sun streamed down upon them, but not to make them uncomfortably hot. They said little, though they noticed many things, and stopped now and then to watch a waterfall or listen to a bird song.

They had passed through the woods and were now on the more rocky slopes. Some days these looked dazzlingly white, other days they were blue, and sometimes, if you looked from the valley, they were wreathed in a magic mist that made then seem very far off and translucent, as though they were made of fine gossamer and you could float through them on the merest breath of a summer’s breeze.

Today the rocks were deep purple, and as they climbed, Paul could see black streaks running zig-zag down the slopes. Each step brought clearer vision, and soon he recognised the black streaks as fissures and clefts, some wide enough for a man to slip through.

At length they paused on a ledge of rock worn smooth by many winters. Contentedly Paul gazed down into the valley. Little was visible from this spot but the dark band of trees above the village, and, far below, the coastline that traced intricate patterns of sea, island and jagged inlet. The sand gleamed white against the silver and deep blue water but from this distance the rushing of the waves was only a whisper.

Paul turned and found Mr. Nogard gazing intently at him. His eyes! He had never noticed them before; they glowed in the brilliant mountain sunlight. Golden they shone, rich and radiant and Paul thought of cornfields rippling in the warm breeze, of church bells in a summer twilight, of racing hot from the sands into the shimmering cool sea, laughing and shouting with Bill and the others. He thought of the organ music that lingered long after the crowds had drifted away after Sunday Mass; and as he gazed into the dragon's golden eyes, he smiled.

The dragon! There he rested, his red and gold scales glinting in the sunlight. Mr. Nogard, friend of the village, was Estrogard, a noble dragon in search of a friend.

For six months of the year he lived on the mountain, coming down to the village in the daytime and returning at dusk. The other six months he spent visiting other dragons in their lairs all over the world. He had to live like a human being when he went among men, because people are very easily frightened. If he had flown from the mountainside and walked along their high street, however slender and superbly crested he was, people just would not have liked it. They would have run inside their houses, bolted the doors and put on double locks, then phoned for the fire, ambulance and police. Perhaps the most adventurous children would have sneaked out of a window, down a drainpipe, after dark to investigate; but even they would have only wanted to throw stones and bottles at him, so that they could be known as the Dragon-killers.

Unfortunately, dragons have got a bad name for breathing fire and destruction, and for carrying off human beings to devour in their lairs. This is not quite true. Dragons are lonely and have, admittedly, carried off people, but only for company. The trouble has been with the people who were so scared at the sight of such splendidly powerful creatures that they usually died of heart failure long before they ever reached the dragon's lair.

In great disappointment a dragon would often turn to hoarding treasure, particularly gold and jewels. Gold is beautiful, especially when worked by a craftsman, but it has a strange power; once a dragon casts his eyes on gold he finds himself enslaved. All his thoughts are on his precious treasure and he will only go out for short snatches, usually at night, perhaps to steal more jewels; but he is always anxious, anxious to be back in his cave, snug with the hoard.

Estrogard knew all this. Once he had been loved by a beautiful firebird who, at the end of her life, had been swept up into the sky to become the brightest constellation. He was heartbroken to lose her, but she had left a tiny feather with him that still burned with her fire. She had told him to search among the sons of men until he found someone to whom he could pass on her fire, and for centuries he had roamed the earth. Everywhere the story was the same: no one stopped to ask what the dragon wanted; no one thought a dragon had a heart.

But now Paul was smiling. Stars were in his eyes. Estrogard caught his breath, then suddenly his long and slender frame uncoiled. Red he flashed in the sunlight, his golden crest glittered as he tossed his head, proud of the rich fire that streamed from his throat. Then a swish of the tail and Paul was swept up high and set down, breathless, on the red scales between the golden wings. Up and up they soared till the powerful wings stopped beating and Paul stood beside Estrogard on the summit of their mountain. His hand was on the dragon's crest, and as they looked out together, fire and laughter rippled over the valley.

# Estrogard's Lair

The entrance to Estrogard's lair was extremely well concealed. A narrow rib of brilliant white quartz ran a little way down the mountain just below the summit on the other side from the valley. Estrogard pressed this gently with one of his golden claws and it slid quietly down on two hinges, to reveal a glassy chute fashioned of opal, flashing green and pink as it caught the mountain sun.

"I was going to cut steps for you last night," Estrogard said, "but then I thought you'd probably prefer the slide. No danger of splinters here."

"You were right," laughed Paul. "Head first, or feet first?"

"Whichever you like, but I'll go first, I like to receive my friends in state."

A chute is, obviously, the most convenient way

for a dragon to go downstairs when there is no room for flying. Estrogard folded his talons under him, and, in a streak of red and gold he had reached the bottom and was coiling himself gracefully, awaiting his guest. Paul took a deep breath – he wasn't going to waste a slide like this; head first or nothing. Stars seemed to whirl around his head as he swept down the opal chute. Then, when he thought he would have to brake if he was to avoid collapsing in an embarrassed heap beside the princely dragon, he found himself being lifted and set upright in front of Estrogard. A rainbow had curled itself round him, and after performing this service was now returning to make an archway so that they could pass into the palace.

For a moment Paul felt a misgiving. Could this beautiful creature really be his friend, Mr. Nogard, who wore the long black coat and would sit for hours whittling sticks to toast crumpets? Could all the splendour of the opal and the rainbow and starlight be meant for him, or was he just a clumsy intruder who would be tolerated politely for a while and then, with infinite courtesy, be sent on his way again, never to repeat the experience?

The dragon was looking at him. In a flash his doubts were all dispelled as he understood the message in the golden eyes.

"Right?" asked Estrogard.

"Great," said Paul, and for a second time that day he gazed at his friend and smiled.

The ceiling of the room they moved into was

fairly high and hung with spider's webs, perpetually silver as when they were first spun in the mountain sunlight and carried here by Estrogard more than a hundred years before. Dew-drops danced and sparkled on them, for he had managed to capture an early morning sunbeam – a difficult feat, as sunbeams are notoriously slippery and elusive. He had skilfully arranged the sunbeam's normal position in a niche high up in the wall, so that the whole room could have radiant sunlight all the time and the spider's webs be shown off to their best advantage. It would have been cruel, however, to imprison a sunbeam, and Estrogard had no trace of cruelty in his nature. So there were no bars or panes of glass for her to beat against, and she would often dart around the room, or streak through the palace playing with the rainbows and the starlight, and creating new forms of light far more beautiful than the most sophisticated firework display.

But she never tried to escape. There was plenty of opportunity for her to do so when Estrogard went in and out. Once he even took her curled like a scarf round his neck all the way down to the village on one of those nippy days just at the end of summer. He wanted to give her the chance to fly away and join her brothers and sisters; but she clung to him all day, warming all the people she met but never leaving him. It was then he realised that she would never grow up; she would always stay with him and give him perpetual sunlight, and he, in turn, would care for her as a child.

Now as they walked about the room she quivered with excitement, then leapt down from her height and danced until it seemed as though there were a thousand sunbeams flashing and spinning in delight. And when they moved from room to room she stayed with them, weaving in and out between them, hanging around Paul's neck, or resting like a golden ball on Estrogard's shoulder.

Paul was too dazzled to notice everything, and he was only vaguely aware that the stars which had whirled round him as he came in belonged to some great store of starlight somewhere within Estrogard's home. But suddenly he stopped dead. From behind a door that leered like an ancient, knotted tree-trunk, he could hear the sound of weeping – stifled moans, heartbreaking sobs, shrill voices raised in fear and anger. Once more doubt clutched at his heart. Who was imprisoned in there? What was happening to them? And could it – could it be that he himself might be about to join them? His head swam at the incredible thought. He closed his eyes. No! No! The dragon was good; he was his friend; there must be some explanation.

"Paul." The voice of Estrogard broke in on his fear, warm and steady. "Don't be afraid. There's nobody else here but ourselves."

"Then what . . . ?" Paul began, but was unable to finish. Estrograd knew what he wanted to say.

"Come, I'll show you."

He pushed open the heavy door and the clamouring voices became more strident, more insistent. Yet the room was empty and dark.

"Hush!" he called, and the lamentation gradually subsided, then ceased.

"Come, sit down with me, Paul." The dragon coiled himself in the centre of the room and drew Paul to sit on one of the coils, resting against his wing. "Have you even wondered what happens to your words and laughter, where they go when they leave you?"

"Yes," said Paul. "I've often listened and listened when the music is finished in the church; the sounds seem to hang among the beams and I feel sad when they fly away at last. I wish I could hold them and make them play forever."

"That's exactly how I feel about them, too," said Estrogard, pleased that they both had the same ideas. "And I've found a way to hold them. All the sounds from the village float up here, and if I didn't stop them they would be carried away, scattered through the mountains and over the sea, and eventually they would become lost sounds. So every evening after sunset, I go out and gather them in my wings. All the tears and the sorrows I put in one room, all the happiness and the music in another. I take the tears and entwine them with the laughter; I take the angry words and mingle them with love words. The bird's song and the children's voices and the organ music wind in and out all night, till at last a new melody is spun from the lost sounds. Then, in the morning before dawn, I slip down to the village and my nightingale sings to the sleeping villagers the song that has been born from all their joys and sorrows."

Paul was very still. "No wonder," he said at last. "That's why the nightingale says so much. I always knew she has more to say than the other birds. And is that why people in our village always wake up happy?"

"They wake up happy if they can hear the nightingale."

"And if they're asleep?"

"Their hearts are awake."

"But some of the old people are deaf. Are there people with deaf hearts?"

"I'm afraid there are a few. They begin by being too busy to stop and listen, then they forget what it was they were listening for; they hear it but don't recognise it; or they think it's a waste of time. Then they fill their hearts with other things. In the end they become stone deaf."

"Do you think that might happen to me?"

Estrogard suddenly looked very grave. "I hope not, Paul. Oh, I hope not."

They were getting serious. The dragon smiled and flicked his tail a little. The movement sent a tickle through Paul's toes and he wriggled and laughed.

"That's better. Now listen to this." Estrogard pushed a door Paul hadn't noticed and suddenly waves and torrents of happy laughter broke over them. Almost as suddenly it ceased and the voice of a bird swept them up into its melody – but Paul couldn't let it finish.

"That's us!" he cried, jumping to his feet, "You and me, last night, and the thrush! It's us!"

Estrogard had uncoiled and was standing, flickers of fire dancing in his open jaws. He was laughing quietly.

"What are you going to make out of that?" Paul asked.

"Make out of it? It's staying as it is. It's perfect."

They both laughed excitedly, then Paul said, "Wouldn't the people in the village feel happier if they heard it?"

"They'll hear it. They'll hear it every time we're down there – if they care to listen. Now it's getting late. We must have something to eat and then I'll take you home."

"Late." What an odd word it sounded. Late and early hadn't seemed to matter here; it was all sunlight and starlight and excitement. And now he'd have to go home.

"When can you come again?"

"Again?" That was better. Paul's eyes lit up once more. "I think I could come tomorrow," he said. "And the next day if the heat lasts. But after that we start to make the hay."

"Well, then, tomorrow and the next day. Until the heatwave is over."

They were eating something quite quickly. Paul couldn't recognise what it was; and he wasn't very hungry anyway; then they stood up.

Paul looked around him as he waited. "How do

we get out?" he asked, remembering the slippery entrance.

"Just sit on my back and you'll see." Once again the rainbow appeared and lifted the boy to his orginal perch between the dragon's wings. The little sunbeam streaked in and wrapped herself around his arm.

"She wants you to come back," said Estrogard. "The place is happier when you're here."

Several stars meteored around the pair, as if to show how much they agreed, and Paul held out both his arms, waving to them all as the dragon's wings spread out and they began to rise. The high vault opened slowly, mountain daylight streamed in, and soon the boy and the dragon were flying down the mountainside.

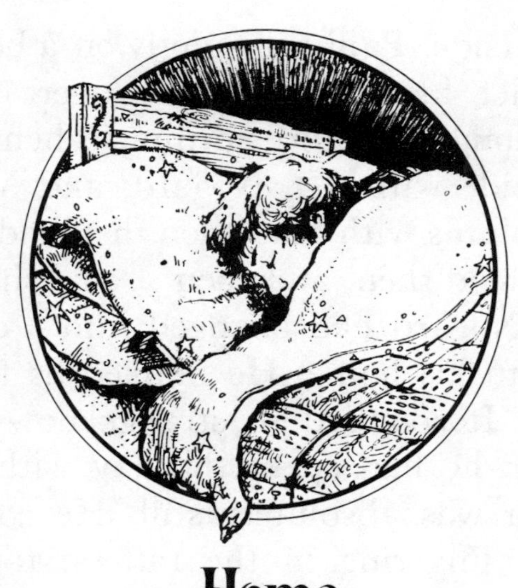

# Home

The evening was cooler as Paul walked along the street to his home, and the villagers were out, reviving after the intense heat of the day. Old Wheezy was sitting on a bench outside the church. Paul stopped; he always had a few words with Old Wheezy. "How are you doing, then?" he shouted. The old man nodded – though he was deaf, he loved people to talk to him.

"Still coughing, then?" He was wheezing as a matter of course. Everything was still the same. "I must be going home. Goodbye." Old Wheezy smiled as Paul trotted off.

Passing the church he decided to go in for a few minutes. He pushed the heavy door and slipped into the dim little building. The air smelt faintly of incense and candle-grease; the place was cool after the heat outside. Paul sat quietly on a bench at the back and let his mind wander over the day. It seemed so long since the morning. Then he had sat on the hillside with Mr. Nogard; and Mr. Nogard had eaten plums with him; then they had walked up the hillside and then, and then . . . he shut his eyes. Then Mr. Nogard had changed into a dragon and taken him to his home. He blinked as the thought penetrated. It sounded so strange now as he was sitting here: he had spent the day with a dragon. The church was absolutely still. He could almost hear music lingering in the rafters; tomorrow he would hear the nightingale by his window. Yes, it was all true, it happened; he didn't know why it had happened, but he didn't need a reason. Happily he slipped out of the bench, bobbed in front of the altar and ran out into the street and home.

"Hallo, Paul," said his mother as he went in. "Where have you been all day?"

"With Mr. Nogard. We went up the mountain together."

"Did you go far up?"

"Yes, all the way."

"All the way? In the sun?"

"Yes, but it wasn't hot."

"But I hope you weren't in the sun all day."

"Oh no – we went to where he lives."

"That's good. I hope he gave you something to eat."

"Yes, we had something before I came home."

How odd it all sounded – as if he'd been to afternoon tea with one of the other boys in the village. Would his mother understand if he explained exactly what had happened? He tried to imagine what he would say:

"Mr. Nogard's a dragon really, and he's got a cave in the mountain, and there's a rainbow there, and a sunbeam that moves, and he collects all the sounds from the village. . . ."

No. For some reason it came out wrong. It just sounded like a rather clumsy fairy tale. His mother wouldn't believe it, and he didn't blame her, really. You'd have to have been there to know what it was like. Talking about it made it sound ridiculous.

All the same he spent the rest of the evening thinking about it, turning the words over and over in his mind. He wanted to tell everyone how wonderful the dragon was and what marvellous things he had in his lair.

"You're very quiet, Paul. Are you sure you're all right?" his mother asked.

"Yes, I'm fine."

"Well, you're not eating much supper."

"I just had some before I came home."

"What did you have?"

"Oh, we had some stuff. I don't know what it was."

"I don't suppose he cooks much for himself, Mr. Nogard, living all on his own like that. You're honoured, going to his house. What's it like, anyway? Plenty of cobwebs, I'll be bound."

Again it was on the tip of his tongue to tell her all

about the place – the chute, the stars, the sunbeam – but something stopped him. How could his mother possibly imagine the ceiling covered with spider's webs? To her they would simply be dusty cobwebs.

"He's got a very nice home."

"Nice! You're like your father. I don't suppose you even noticed whether he had a front door or a back door."

"Oh I did. He had a . . . a front entrance and a middle. . . . entrance – for going out."

"Exit is the word you're fishing for," interrupted Bill, Paul's elder brother.

"Don't start squabbling now." Father joined in quickly to prevent any heated tempers; he knew Paul was apt to retaliate when teased. But not this evening. Nothing could annoy him after such a day.

"Can I go out for a bit, Mum?"

"Out? I should think you've been out enough for one day. You can wash up the dishes and empty the rubbish. Then bed."

"O.K."

"Are you all right, Paul?" Bill's surprise was genuine. Usually there was a fight about the washing up, Paul strongly resisted.

"Course I'm all right. Why?"

"Just wondered. You wouldn't like to wipe up too?"

"Oh hey, that's not fair. Wiping up's your share."

"Pack it up there." Their father's voice cut in

abruptly once again.

"All right, all right," Bill soothed. "Just thought you were looking for a good deed."

The job was done. Paul dried his hands and went over to his mother. "Good night, Mum."

"Good night, love. I'll be up later."

Paul gave Bill a brotherly kick on his way out of the door, and there was a brief scuffle.

"I told you two to pack it up."

"Night Dad."

"Night," grunted their father.

When his mother called in later it was dark, but Paul was lying awake.

"Are you not asleep yet?"

"I'm not tired yet." There was a little pause, then "Mum?"

"Yes love?"

"Mum, you know I said I was with Mr. Nogard today."

"Yes."

"Well, Mr. Nogard's really a dragon."

"Is he? Well I never!"

"And he lives in a beautiful cave made of shining stone."

"Does he, love? Well, just you go to sleep and dream all about it."

"And we played with rainbows and a sunbeam." Paul's voice was becoming drowsy. "It was a lovely day."

"I'm very glad. Now you can go fast asleep. Goodnight."

"Night Mum."

His mother walked quietly out and closed the door softly.

"I'm a bit worried about Paul," she said to her husband when she went downstairs.

"What's the matter?"

"I think he's got a touch of sunstroke. He'd better stay in tomorrow."

Back up on the mountain, Estrogard was pensively watching the sun set. Behind him the sky was already dark but he was looking into an inferno; fire burned the sky as the sun sank into the sea. A late rabbit loped across the tufts of coarse mountain grass that grew on the slope near the cave.

"Evenin', sir," he said as he came up to the dragon.

"Evening."

"See you had company today."

"Yes – a friend of mine from the village."

The rabbit settled down on his haunches for a chat.

"Nice to see a bit of life up here now and again. Reckon you must get fair lonely living here all by yourself."

The dragon laughed a little. "Yes, it has been lonely at times. But it won't be any more now."

"Coming up again, then, is he?"

"Yes, I hope so."

"Good thing, too. I was just saying to my missus the other day, I felt sorry for you living up here, no relations popping in and out, no kiddies around.

We rabbits – well, you know," he laughed. "There are always kids around with us, and so many relations we don't know who's brothers and who's cousins. And I was just saying to my missus, pity he's so big. I'd like to have him in one day, but he'd never get in – or out. No offence, of course, sir."

"None taken," Estrogard smiled. "It was an extremely kind thought, all the same. Thank you for thinking it."

"Be a good day tomorrow, I reckon. Like today."

"Maybe."

"Well, I must be hopping. See you tomorrow."

"See you."

He was gone, loping home in the darkness to his burrow, overcrowded with rabbits young and old.

Again Estrogard looked out to the sea. Daylight was almost gone; a brilliant path of shimmering red gold led straight across the water into the heart of the sinking sun.

"Be a good day tomorrow, I reckon. Like today."

The dragon closed his eyes. "Maybe," he whispered.

# An Early Start

Cool, still, the morning lay asleep in the valley. Stars and moon were beginning very gently to fade; faint rays of dawn were about to turn the world from black to grey. Through the darkness a nightingale's clear song thrilled the stillness.

She sang close to Paul's window, and at the first note he sat up, instantly awake. He listened to her until, drenched with the music, he remembered each second of the previous day, and knew that everything about it had been real. Within a few minutes he was out of bed, dressed, and ready to go out into the cool dawn. Instinctively he felt that his mother would prevent him from going out all day again, so he decided to leave now, before anyone awoke. He scribbled a note:

"Dear Mum, I'll be back this evening. Don't

worry. Paul."

To go downstairs was too dangerous – she'd be sure to wake up. The best thing was to leave the note on his pillow where she'd find it when she came to call him, and slip out through the window.

The house was not a high one – really it was a cottage; Paul and Bill slept in the loft which had been divided into two rooms. He clambered over the windowsill and dropped lightly onto the turf below. After this he had to walk across the fields at the back of the house; to leave by the front gate would have been more direct, but the gravel crunching underfoot would have betrayed him.

The fields were heavy with dew, and he walked barefoot carrying his sandals. At a safe distance from the house he joined the road which ran along the bay for a while, before rising towards the mountain, away from the sea. Again this morning a heavy mist lay on the water; the tide was full in, and ripples lapped the rocky shore next to the road.

When he had walked as far as the edge of the forest he began to feel hungry.

He was a healthy boy and had not eaten much the day before, from sheer excitement. He looked up at the still darkened sky; there would be a long time to wait before Mr. Nogard appeared, he thought. He would have liked to meet him half-way, but no child ever went into the forest alone; even adults were chary, and only ventured alone in cases of emergency. Mr. Nogard was the only person who appeared to have no fear and would come and go with ease.

As Paul leaned against a gnarled oak tree, it occurred to him that this was just the season for blackberries; most of the bushes were in the forest itself, but there were enough on the fringes to provide him with a good breakfast. When he eventually returned to the oak, he was surprised to find Mr. Nogard already sitting down smoking a pipe as if it had been broard daylight, instead of scarcely dawn.

"Thought you might be up early," he said as he greeted Paul with a nod.

"I thought I'd better get out before they woke up. I didn't tell anyone, just left a note."

"Did you say you'd be with me?"

"No, but my mum will guess that."

"Had enough to eat?"

Actually Paul felt rather sick; he had eaten every blackberry he could lay his hands on, without stopping to consider whether he'd had enough or not.

"Yes, thanks."

"I brought a few odds and ends, but we can have them later. You look a bit patchy. Here, wipe your face. We're going somewhere very special today."

Paul wiped his face with the proffered handkerchief – at least it was better than having his mother hold his head down and scrub till his eyes smarted. Mr. Nogard was still smoking his pipe, and eyeing Paul a little critically. "O.K?"

"Yes thanks."

"Well, you'll do. Come on." Up he sprang, suddenly full of energy, and together they walked into the wood, swiftly and with light steps, full of excitement at the thought of the day ahead. Not many birds were awake even yet, and the two hardly spoke. Even the trees were asleep, though occasionally Paul thought he saw one stretch and shake its branches, and sigh, as if yawning deep. It was so dark that he couldn't be sure; he'd ask Mr. Nogard later.

When they emerged at the other side of the forest the sky was grey and rapidly growing paler. Silver streaks were beginning to take on a faintly golden glow; soon the sun would be up. Here they were above the mist which swathed the village and hung upon the sea. Within a few hours, that, too, would have dispersed, and today, again, the villagers would wilt in their parlours and kitchens, trying to escape from the heat.

Now they were at the Dragon Rock. Paul had christened it that as he lay in bed the previous evening. Twice now his friend had been transformed beside him at the same place, and Paul had no idea how it happened. One moment there was a man in a black coat, the next moment there was a dragon. This time he would be prepared – he would watch. But in vain. Although he kept his eyes on Mr. Nogard all the time, there was no sign of a gradual transformation. Now he was a man, and now he was a dragon – and once Paul was looking at his friend Estrogard, it seemed as if there never had been any change.

Estrogard who knew what was in Paul's mind

laughed loudly. "So you want to know how it's done, do you?"

"Yes, I want to know that, and I want to know – everything, and especially I. . . ."

"One thing at a time. Now, up on my back."

Again the brilliant tail coiled around Paul, lifted him and set him down.

"Comfy?"

"Uh-huh. Now will you tell me, please?"

"Right. First question."

"Why can't I see you changing from Mr. Nogard into the red dragon?"

Again the dragon's laughter pealed out across the valley, as he soared up towards the mountain peak with the boy.

"Why? Because I don't change, you change."

If Paul had not been sitting on the broadest part of the dragon's back, with two strong wings to protect him, he would have slipped off with shock. As it was he lurched to one side and clutched tightly to the golden crest.

"Steady now. Watch it. We're going for a long trip today. Don't fall off before we've even started."

Paul righted himself, and then in a moment they were landing near the quartz slab, now glinting in the early sun.

"We won't stop for long here. We'll just pick up a few provisions and then we'll be off."

Paul had slipped from the dragon's back and was examining himself, craning his neck to see his back, and feeling himself cautiously.

"What did you mean? I'm no different. Where's the change?"

Estrogard's laughter was gentle this time. "It's in your eyes and your heart, Paul. You have the gift of being able to see me as I really am."

Paul understood, then, what his friend meant. He couldn't have explained it to anyone, but deep down inside him he understood exactly. And he understood dimly that it would be impossible for him ever to use this gift in the village. There he would see only Mr. Nogard. Later he would ask Estrogard why.

The little sunbeam had only just awoken. She stretched prettily as Paul wandered into the spiders' web room, then slipped from her perch and drowsily wrapped herself around his neck.

"Is she coming with us?" Paul called, stroking her gently.

"No – we're going too far today. She'd get tired. It's all right, she won't mind being left behind. She keeps the cave warm and bright while I'm gone."

"You can't come with us today, but we'll take you another day," whispered Paul, then lifted the sunbeam from his shoulders, climbed on a high stool and softly placed her back in her niche. She was fast asleep.

"Are you ready?" Estrogard was standing beneath the vault. Paul ran from the sunbeam room, climbed Estrogard's back, and in a moment they were out on the mountain.

"Where are we going?"

"Visiting. I've some very special friends who live across the sea, and I want them to meet you."

"Is it far?"

"Not by air, We'll be there before noon."

The vault had closed with a slow rumbling sound. The mountain lay undisturbed once more. A few scattered boulders threw long shadows, and the rock slopes looked rich green in the early morning sun.

"Wait! Wait!" Paul heard an urgent squeak and Estrogard turned his head to see the rabbit of last night hopping from tuft to tuft towards them, somewhat hampered by a large basket slung round his neck.

"The missus . . . the missus . . ." he gulped breathlessly.

"It's all right, old chap. Take your time," said Estrogard, "Get your breath back."

"The missus thought you'd like these, seeing as you had company again. We didn't think you'd be up so early though. I was just going to leave them at the front door for a surprise. Lucky I caught you."

"It certainly was lucky," said Estrogard, "We're off on a long trip today. Look, Paul – a present from the rabbit family – from one very select branch of the family, I should say."

He relieved the rabbit of his cumbersome load, and passed the basket up to Paul, to whom the converation had, so far, been nothing more than squeaks and growls. It has never occurred to him as strange that he could understand the speech of a dragon; he simply took it for granted that he should understand his friend, Estrogard. But now he realised with a little pang of disappointment that the dragon and the rabbit were having a conversation that he could not share. His attention was soon distracted, however, by the contents of the basket.

"Strawberries! And a honeycomb! Look Estrogard – the basket's full of strawberries, big ones!"

The basket was heavy with fruit, glistening fresh and cold, for a few of the younger rabbits had been out early to pick them. The honeycomb had been carefully wrapped in lettuce leaves from Mr. Rabbit's specially cultivated patch – "so's not to lose all the honey before they even start out," Mrs. Rabbit had said. And she had slipped in a couple of peeled and pointed sticks for spearing the strawberries, "You get so messy with honey"; and damp, spongy moss "for wiping your paws afterwards." Just to look at the basket, you could tell it had been packed by somebody's mother.

Estrogard was really thrilled, but he didn't say much. "Please thank your wife and family. We'll enjoy all this on the way. It's a good start for a happy day. Goodbye."

And then they were off, rising slowly, circling the mountain, until the farewell squeaks of the rabbit were lost in the distance, and they seemed to be flying straight for the risen sun.

# An Accident

Paul had never been further from home than the town twelve miles away, and then the journey had been made on foot, driving the cattle to market with the other village boys; except occasionally, when his father took him in the battered but serviceable old car, leaving Bill to see to the animals. These occasions were becoming increasingly rare, for Paul had a certain gentle way of guiding the cattle, and with him they always arrived sooner and in far better temper than with Bill or any of the farm hands. The cows seemed to understand what he said to them, although the only answer they ever gave was "moo".

This was his first long journey, and as he soared upwards and out across the sea he was noticing everything, and imagined himself telling all his friends in the village the next day. They met several swallows, gulls flying quite low, a lark or two, and most of them would perch on Estrogard's crest and travel with them for a time. It was like aerial hitch-hiking; and though Paul couldn't work out their sign, it was quite evident that the birds and the dragon were on very good terms. They chatted cheekily to Estrogard, and a blackbird sang a serenade that made up to Paul for not being able to follow the conversation. When they passed over land the birds would leave them saying what must have been "thanks for the lift" to Estrogard, and resting for a moment on Paul's shoulder or hand to give a nod and a farewell twitter; the blackbird left behind a glossy feather from his tail.

After the blackbird had flown off they were alone for a time. Land was far behind them and there was not much to look at now – sparkling blue sea flecked with foam below, shimmering blue sky flecked with cloud above. Paul began to feel hungry.

"Would you like something to eat?" he asked Estrogard.

"I was wondering when you'd realise you were hungry," chuckled the dragon. "Put out your left hand – onto my wing. Now slip your hand under the fold in the scales. That's right. Found anything?"

"Yes! Crumpets!"

"Don't pull them all out at once or you won't be able to manage with the basket as well. Just take a couple for a start. Now, if you're very careful, you can lean forward and I'll toast them for you."

"I can't manage; the basket's in the way."

"Sit tight" – and with that, the end of the dragon's tail flicked forward, hooked the basket from Paul's grasp, and remained coiled just below the right wing, so that Paul could reach the strawberries and honey when he was ready for them.

Cautiously he began to crawl forward on his tummy, along the dragon's neck until he could grip the crest and lean forward safely. He held a crumpet at Estrogard's open jaws, a little nervous of getting his fingers burnt.

"That's one done."

Amazingly it was – toasted on both sides while Paul was wondering when the fire was going to start issuing forth. He held the second one down – that was ready now, too.

"Do you want honey on yours?"

Naturally Estrogard wanted honey and strawberries, so for the next few minutes Paul was kept busy sticking the strawberries to the crumpet with honey. Then he had to feed Estrogard who was concentrating on flying. By himself he didn't mind doing several things at once with wings, talons and tail but with Paul on his back, he wasn't taking any risks.

By the time he had toasted half a dozen of the crumpets Paul was beginning to feel a little overconfident. Now he was not inching his way cautiously but swinging his legs expertly from the back to the neck. Estrogard sensed the growing recklessness in the boy.

"You've had enough now Paul; save some for later."

"Just this one," said Paul, quickly snatching a last crumpet from the wing and sitting on the dragon's neck.

Sit down!" cried Estrogard sharply. Shocked by his hardness, Paul went to sit quickly, lost his balance and fell. He was hurtling through the air and the sea seemed to rush angrily to meet him. He couldn't breathe or cry out, but gasped little frightened whimpers. Then he was seized roughly by a strong, muscular coil that gripped his waist, nearly squeezing all the breath from his lungs. He was being lifted again into the air, and clung with both hands to the rough hide of his rescuer. His immediate danger was over, but who was he with now? His eyes had been tightly closed in terror but curiosity was stronger now than fear and he opened them. Relief flooded his body as he recognised the shiny red and gold scales of Estrogard; he closed his eyes once again, pressed his face against the dragon's body, and began to cry.

Estrogard, too, was relieved when he felt Paul shaking with sobs. He had feared that the shock of the fall and the violence of the rescue might have been too much for the boy. There was a long way to go before they reached any land, however, and he was doubtful of the power of his tail to carry Paul all the way. The child's uncontrollable sobbing made the flying all the more difficult and for the second time, anxiety lent harshness to the dragon's words.

"Stop that, Paul. Keep still or you'll fall again."

Stunned, Paul broke off in the middle of a sob, and for a while gasped and gulped until he had regained control, too frightened to disobey. This was an Estrogard he had never met before, this grim creature who issued commands and hadn't one kind word to say. After all, he'd nearly been drowned; you'd think someone who was his friend would be nice to him when he was crying. He didn't often, after all. Estrogard had never seen him cry before. And he'd nearly been killed. Estrogard would have been mighty sorry then. Well, if that's how he was going to be, then let him.

Without realising it, while he was having these rebellious thoughts, Paul was rapidly recovering from his shock, and soon he had examined his position and was able to say to Estrogard.

"I could quite easily climb onto your back from here."

"Stay exactly where you are and keep still."

An old wound was reopening – one Estrogard had received a few centuries ago when he fought with Thorgild. It was his weakest spot, and now the ice that had entered in then, began to jab and cruelly work its way along the coiled tail. Ice, freezing the warm, breathing body.

The dragon was growing tired, and the hot sun did not make flight any easier. They should soon sight the island that was their destination; he scanned the horizon – would it never appear? If he could have seen a dolphin below, he would have swooped down to the surface of the water, and used the dolphin's back as a mounting block for Paul. Any other solution would be too dangerous. He did not dare risk losing his precious load again. The numbness was stealthily creeping upwards. Not a dolphin in sight; not a speck of land.

Petulantly Paul clung on behind. It looked so simple; all he needed to do was to clasp the dragon's body with both hands, swing up his feet, and hanging upside down, work his way along until he reached the wings; then if Estrogard would swing his tail to the front, he could step from the tail to his original position between the wings. Simple and obvious. Estrogard was just being awkward and pig-headed.

A powerful bellow, such as he had never heard before broke in on his angry thoughts, and he felt the dragon's body quiver with effort. Estrogard had seen, far, far above, a tiny black speck that he knew must be an eagle. If only the eagle could hear from that distance! Again he bellowed, deep, thunderous and resonant. Fire flashed from his jaws in an urgent appeal. Would the eagle notice, so far away? Anxiously Estrogard stared upward; but the tiny speck seemed to grow tinier; the bird must be flying away, soaring even higher. Still he gazed; he would not believe that help was receding from them. He had no strength left now to cry out again – all his energies were directed to keeping in flight; but the eagle must come.

And then – glinting golden in the sun, the bird's form grew larger and larger as the eagle winged his powerful way down towards the dragon, now dangerously near the water's surface.

Paul saw none of this but he heard what was evidently an urgent interchange between Estrogard and some raucous bird. Within a few moments he was seized unceremoniously by the shoulders, released by the dragon's tail, tossed slightly into the air and caught around the waist by two powerful talons. Soon the eagle was flying high and swiftly away with the boy, leaving Estrogard below and far behind.

Watching them go Estrogard felt sad. What a way to part with Paul. He had been terrified by the fall and now he was being carried away by an eagle without a word of explanation. And the last words they had exchanged had been angry ones. Paul's last memory of his dragon friend would not be a very pleasant one to cherish. But he would make it up to him – there was still something Estrogard could do even at a distance and in his weak state; he would give Paul the gift of being able to understand the speech of all living creatures.

Now he felt happier. Paul would be safe – the eagle would see to that – and in no time he would come to understand. He did not feel so weak now that his tail no longer had to bear the boy's weight; but he was more exhausted than he realised. His eyes kept roving down to the sea that seemed to lure him with a promise of rest. This was a snare and he knew it, for an earth or an air-dragon can only float for a time on the surface, he cannot swim; and once on the water he needs great strength in his wings to rise again, for there is no solid base to help him into flight. Estrogard's wings were weary, his body was growing cold, yet he dared not give in just yet. He had no idea how long it would be before the eagle could arrange a rescue, and if he yielded to the temptation to touch the sea, he doubted he would ever rise again. Doggedly his wings beat on; and yet he had to face the fact that if there was no help soon he would have to give in; and it would be farewell to Paul and to the sunlight. The sea would extinguish his fire.

# An Eagle, a Gryphon and a Unicorn

When Paul realised that he was being carried away from the dragon, a tumult of thoughts raced through his mind. Estrogard had known all those bad thoughts of his and was disgusted, didn't want to have anything more to do with him, was letting a great vicious bird carry him off. But Estrogard wasn't like that; even if he did know what Paul had been thinking, he still loved him. Yet why then was he so uncomfortably being clutched by this eagle? And where was he going? It suddenly occurred to Paul with horror that he might never see Estrogard again. Now he knew how much he cared about his beautiful red dragon, who looked so pathetically small far below. He cried out to the eagle:

"Where are you taking me? Why couldn't I stay with my dragon?"

"Consider yourself extremely fortunate, my young man, that a royal eagle was passing your way. No other bird would have the strength to do what I am doing for you."

The eagle's voice was rasping and his expression supercilious. Obviously he was used to deferential treatment, but Paul was in no mood for playing the courtier.

"Where are you taking me?" he repeated. "And what's going to happen to Estrogard?" His voice was rising in anxiety as he began very dimly to understand what his situation might mean.

"You might well ask," snapped the eagle. "You might well ask. He's quite exhausted having to hold you up. I shouldn't be at all surprised if he's drowned before we get a lifeline out to him. Not at all surprised."

So, that was it. That was the whole story. Estrogard was in real danger, but he had taken care that Paul should be saved. Frantically he scanned the sea for a glimpse of the red and gold dragon, but there was nothing to be seen except endless blue flecked with white. Miserably he wondered, with a dull hope, whether they had left Estrogard so far behind that he was out of sight. The other alternative was too horrible to imagine, and he closed his eyes to try to shut out the thought.

Other thoughts crowded his mind. If only . . . oh, if only he had not been so stupid! He hadn't wanted that last crumpet; he just wanted to show off by standing on the dragon's back. As if he needed to show off to Estrogard! Well, the basket would be well and truly empty now. Wryly he hoped that the fishes liked strawberries and honey. The rabbit came into his mind. Would he ever get back to tell the rabbit he was sorry he'd lost his basket? And would Estrogard ever see the mountain again? He imagined himself returning alone, standing helpless outside the dragon's lair, unable to tell the little sunbeam that her master would never be home again. He was choking with tears despite his attempts to fight them back. He didn't want the eagle to know he was crying.

"Oh, do stop snivelling, little boy. It's bad enough having to drag you all this way, without having to listen to you as well. Please do not interrupt my thoughts again. That is the third time an interruption has occurred."

Paul was furious. He wished he could sneeze – that would really shake the eagle. But that might be dangerous. For his own safety's sake he would have to control his anger, lest he be dropped into the sea. He looked down, blinked, looked again. Land! Below them, and not very far below, lay an island. While his eyes had been closed, he had not been aware that they were rapidly descending, and within a few moments they were near enough for the eagle to loosen his clothes and drop the boy onto soft, warm sand.

Then he flew through a few trees to a clearing where Paul could see two stately creatures resting in a dignified pose. It only took a few seconds for the eagle to alert them and they soon emerged from the clearing, dragging a large but light canoe, and hurrying to the shore. At a few yards from Paul they were recognisable; one was a gryphon, the other a unicorn. The latter stepped into the canoe and sat down on his haunches.

"You'd be better on your side," suggested the gryphon. "Then you can hang your head over as a lookout."

The eagle grasped a strong rope from the bows in his beak and the gryphon seized one from the stern. They were poised for flight when Paul ran towards them.

"Wait! Wait! Please take me! I want to come to the rescue too!"

"Go away little boy! You've caused enough trouble for one day. Quite enough." That was the eagle – doubly disgruntled because in speaking to Paul he had to drop the rope.

"Stay here on the island," said a much softer, deep voice. "We won't be long at all, and there's plenty of food on the table. Take anything you want." The gryphon was looking kindly, though solemnly at Paul whose disappointment and fear were obvious. "Don't you worry, my little man, we'll soon have your friend safely here."

"If you waste any more time talking there'll be no friend to bring here!" The eagle was anxious to be on his way.

"Hoist away!" said the unicorn, and the canoe rose, suspended by ropes from the beaks of the eagle and the gryphon who rapidly gathered speed as they hastened to the rescue of the red dragon whom they all loved so well.

Perhaps because he was flying in company now, the eagle found that the return journey was far quicker than his outward flight. It was still quite a long time, however, before the unicorn sighted the dragon below.

"He's there! Due west; start descending now. No time to lose; body floating."

Rapidly eagle and gryphon descended until the canoe was skimming the surface and they drew up alongside an Estrogard who could scarcely flicker his eyes in greeting. Unicorn and eagle weighted the canoe which rocked perilously as the gryphon helped to bundle in the almost powerless dragon. Limply he lay at the bottom of the boat and only managed to mutter hoarsely, "Thanks for being so quick, friends."

Then they were off again, speeding through the waters, while the unicorn steered and the other two provided the power from above.

Paul, meanwhile, was feeling utterly wretched. The whole miserable affair seemed to be entirely his fault, and though the gryphon had tried to be encouraging the eagle's pessimistic anxiety was the more forceful, and the boy was already imagining his friend to be lost. Black despair gnawed at his heart; he forgot his own danger, so far from home, abandoned on an island he knew not where. None of this mattered. If Estrogard was dead he did not care what happened to himself.

Behind him stood a house curiously wrought of carved wood and a table laden with delicious food. Beside him on the beach shells of rare design and delicate colours lay strewn in rich profusion. Above, the brilliantly blue sky hung like a splendid dome. Paul saw none of these, but only the hostile sea that stretched sparkling, calm, yet treacherous before him.

He watched numbly, without hope, for the flying creatures to return. When at last they appeared on the horizon, he could scarcely believe that they were really approaching. He ran to the water's edge and waited in an agony of hope and fear, straining his eyes and every muscle in his body to see whether Estrogard was with them. At times his heart leapt as he thought he saw something red flash in the sun; then he despaired as it disappeared and there were only three forms to be seen.

So it was, until the canoe was dragged ashore and Paul retreated, waiting at a little distance, his heart pounding as if it would burst through his ribs. The gryphon alighted on the sand; the eagle perched on the stern; the unicorn stood in the canoe where he was; all were motionless.

And Estrogard raised his head and flexed his wings, and stepped out, a little wobbly, but without assistance, onto firm land. Paul didn't move. You might have expected that he would run to his friend and tell him he was sorry, and show how glad he was to see him safe. That was exactly what he wanted to do; but something strange inside held him back. He looked at Estrogard and saw, not his friend of the mountainside and the cave, but a lordly creature surrounded by other splendid beasts who had been willing to drop everything to come to his rescue. He felt as if he had strayed into another world where Estrogard was not only at home, but was treated with respect as if he were a prince, or at least someone they had known for a long, long time, and had come to love and honour greatly. And here was he, a boy who had lived only a few years in one small village and knew next to nothing . . . small, foolish, clumsy . . . he took another step backwards, wishing he could melt into the shadows of the trees.

"Aren't you pleased so see me?" the voice was Estrogard's, but the person walking towards Paul, hands outstretched, limping just a little, was Mr. Nogard.

Then Paul did run to him, laughing and crying both at one, and Mr. Nogard caught him up and spun round, swinging the boy off the ground. And when he set Paul down again, he was a dragon, facing his stately friends but standing firmly with Paul beside him.

"Gentlemen," he said, in a most dignified manner, "this young man deserves your very special consideration. May I introduce to you, Paul, my friend."

# Relaxing

It was quite surprising how quickly Paul's appetite had returned. He said very little during the meal that followed Estrogard's safe arrival, for he still felt somewhat overawed by the noble beasts who were his companions. The gryphon sat at the head of the table with Estrogard on his right and Paul on his left. Facing him perched the eagle on a slender carved column. The unicorn at first waited on them, with stately dignity, holding the silver bowls and dishes with one hoof, serving the guests expertly with the other. There were roast potatoes, Yorkshire pudding, and quantities of delicacies such as Paul had never tasted before. The gryphon, acting as host, led the conversation, and Paul noticed that whenever they referred to something of which he was ignorant, the gryphon would courteously explain the details, so that he never felt left out. It was in this way that Paul was able, gradually, to piece together the history of the gryphon and the unicorn – a story as intriguing as the two beasts themselves.

They still behaved with courtly formality even though it was many years since they had left the court. They had been the king's heraldic beasts, but the affectedness and hypocrisy of the people surrounding the king had so disgusted them that they had walked out one day, determined to find a place where they could be themselves, and where they could make people feel they mattered for themselves and not for their wealth or rank or talents. They tried many places – towns, villages, schools, farms, – any place where men gathered, for they were sociable beasts and loved company. But a few weeks in each place was enough to convince them that the paradise they were seeking was not yet discovered. Everywhere, it seemed, people paid more attention to the fact that they were the royal beasts than that they were a gryphon and a unicorn looking for friends. Eventually they had made their way far, far across the sea to this island, believing that they would have to create the perfect land themselves. They hoped that people would come to hear of it, and visit them; then they would have a chance to put their ideals into effect. They told the birds who passed over and frequently stayed with them for long periods to bring the message to the people on the mainland. They built a canoe, light, but large and sturdy, to ferry the people across. But some of the birds were heedless, and forgot the message once they had left behind the warm hospitality of the island; others, more serious, tried to tell men, but their earnest words were mistaken for twittering and the message was never understood.

Occasionally a young man and woman would stand beneath the stars and gaze out to sea, dreaming of a perfect life; but the birds had gone to sleep by that time; they were, after all, only messengers.

Perhaps they should have developed their own publicity; nothing came of the birds' efforts among human beings. They had other visitors, though. Any creature that could swim or fly knew that he or she was welcome on the island. There would be a feast with the kind of food he liked best and after the feasting there would be entertainment. The gryphon would play his lute while the unicorn sang plaintive old airs. Then the guest would contribute in his own way – no one would ever forget a brilliant display given by two swordfish who, in a ritual dance, flashed rays and arcs through a rainbow pool as their swords wove patterns in the sunlight waters.

Yes, every creature loved to visit the gryphon and unicorn's island; and yet Paul sensed a certain loneliness and disappointment about the two of them. They still kept up many of the courtly usages that were of little point any longer. Before the meal they always bowed their heads respectfully in a prayer for the king, refusing to believe the rumours carried by the pigeons that there was no longer king nor court, but a strange man called a president, and a democracy. The table for the meal was laid as if it were in the banqueting hall of the palace. Three wine glasses each, silver drawn up like soldiers, in battalion – "Start at the outside and work in," whispered the unicorn, as Paul wondered what to attack with first – and rose water to cleanse your fingers after a leg or a wing. The damask napkins seemed the most out of place, especially as Paul was the only member of the party who could make use of them for their original purpose.

The unicorn had joined them at the table. He and the gryphon took it in turns to wait at table, even when they dined alone, but they always joined the company once all were served. He sat next to Paul and chatted and told jokes, and, if the conversation were beginning to flow above Paul's head, he would give him another helping of oysters or pickled onions.

At length all were satisfied, and the gryphon considerately suggested that perhaps Estrogard might like a rest after his trying journey. At this, the unicorn eagerly offered to take Paul on a tour of the island. Automatically Paul wondered about the washing up. He looked at the unicorn but there was no suggestion of "washing up" in his eyes. He looked at the eagle. "Can't imagine him doing it," he thought. "I'd better offer. I suppose." And yet no one was making a move, even to stack the dishes. Maybe it wasn't done in these circles. He decided, after all, that perhaps he had better leave his hosts to make the first move – they had very quaint ways, but he would hate to hurt their feelings by interfering.

So he climbed on the unicorn's back and they moved off, slowly, because all the company had eaten enormously, and they were not in an athletic mood. Estrogard, the eagle and the gryphon moved into the house, where the dragon was invited to recline on a softly upholstered couch. There all three stayed, chatting, because Estrogard's mind wasn't tired, only his muscles, and he had come all this way especially to see the gryphon, who for a little while massaged the life back into the drangon's benumbed tail.

"I wanted you to meet my friend, Paul," he said.

"I really don't understand how you can have made such a friend of a little boy," said the eagle, who had been feeling somewhat put out at all the attention Paul was receiving. "Surely there are plenty of perfectly fine beasts or birds whom you could have befriended."

"There may have been," replied Estrogard a little hotly, "but if there were, they took several centuries to show themselves." Then he turned to the gryphon and said, half apologetically, "Of course I have friends among the birds and the beasts as you both have proved today. And I thank you both for saving my life and Paul's. That was true friendship."

The eagle looked somewhat mollified by this recognition of his services, and the gryphon smiled kindly at Estrogard as he sat down and drew on his hookah (he always smoked after dinner).

"We understand, Estrogard, my friend. Everyone loves and honours you for your kindness and graciousness. But your young Paul is different. He wouldn't be able to give any reason for his friendship. To him you're just you – his dragon – and that's all that matters."

Estrogard smiled; but the eagle was still not satisfied. "But why a little boy?"

Estrogard spoke. "No reason at all – except that when I went knocking on people's hearts he was the only one who opened the door and invited me in."

That stumped the eagle; he was effectively silenced for a long while, as the gryphon and Estrogard continued their conversation, the gryphon still half dreaming about his perfect land, Estrogard giving him some practical suggestions for making it effective.

"Why don't you find an island nearer the mainland? I know I've said this before, but I still believe you would attract some people if your island were not so remote."

But the gryphon felt he and his friend, the unicorn, were too old now to move; besides, they would never find a deserted island near the mainland. They had lived away from people for so long now that they preferred to spend the rest of their days as they were.

The afternoon wore lazily on. Now and then,

shrieks and whinnying of laughter would be wafted to the little carved house, as Paul and the unicorn played around the island. Paul had forgotten any fear and was practising all kinds of feats. He even managed to keep a handstand on the unicorn's back while they galloped along the sand. The unicorn was wonderful company, game for anything; full of stories too, and a good listener.

By the end of the afternoon Paul had confided to him all the horror of that morning's journey. He felt better after talking about it, especially when the unicorn assured him that Estrogard would be perfectly well after his rest.

"Dragons don't get really ill," he explained. "They can become exhausted, but a good meal, a rest and a few kind words are enough to make them recover completely. So you've no need to worry about your friend. "And he is my friend," thought Paul proudly. "These others are his friends too, but we're only visiting them. I'm going home with him."

And he sprang up from the sand where they had been relaxing, stripped, and ran splashing into the warm blue sea. The unicorn plunged after him and once again they played happily, the unicorn amusing Paul by catching exotic little fishes on the tip of his horn, asking them riddles and then tossing them back into the water.

At length they returned to join the others, and while Paul rested on a rug beside Estrogard, the gryphon and the unicorn went outside together for a while. The eagle was still there, and Paul still felt slightly hostile towards him, though of course he had to remember that, grumpy though he might be, the eagle was really the hero of the day.

"Ahem." The eagle cleared his throat. "Did you, did you ahem . . . enjoy your afternoon?"

"Me?" asked Paul, surprised to be addressed. Then realising that he sounded rude added hurriedly, "Yes, yes we had a lovely time, thank you." He would have said more, but the eagle had been so sarcastic before about his speaking that he didn't like to risk annoying him again.

"Nice little island – er – this – er don't you think?"

"I think it's beautiful." Curiously he looked up at the eagle. An amazing thought struck him – perhaps the eagle was trying to make friends. He remembered all he owed to him – without the eagle there would be no Paul. He stood up so that he was on a level with the bird's head.

"I'm very sorry for not saying it before, but thank you very much for saving both of us."

"Oh, not at all, not at all," replied the eagle quickly. But his feathers ruffled and fluttered a little, and Paul knew he was pleased. Now he felt ashamed of his previous bad thoughts. Clearly the eagle had only been touchy because he wanted a bit of attention.

"If there's anything I can do for you, just let me know," continued the boy. "I don't suppose I can be much use to someone like you, but you never know."

"Oh, that's very kind of you;" the eagle's voice was gruff. "That's very kind indeed. I'll remember that. Indeed I will."

Then the two hosts returned to say that tea was served, and this time it was the gryphon who poured out the tea from the silver teapot into the bone china cups. Once again it was dignified, stately but still in some way sad. They were eating thin bread and butter in silence when the gryphon and unicorn looked at each other questioningly. The unicorn spoke.

"We were wondering, Estrogard, whether Paul . . ." he trailed off, for the first time at a loss for words.

"You see, Estrogard" continued the gryphon, "Paul is the first human being ever to visit our island, and we wondered if . . ." he looked at the unicorn, appealing for support.

"Maybe he would like to live with us so that our island can at last become the perfect land." There. It was said. Estrogard moved slightly.

"That is something only Paul can decide," he said slowly. All eyes were fixed anxiously on the boy. He felt bewildered. Stay here? It would be fun certainly. The unicorn was good company: there seemed to be plenty to eat and no work to do. He thought of home and all the odd jobs. No washing up here, no arguments, no mother telling him to wash his neck. No mother! But that would be terrible! Never to go back home? His mother would go out of her mind with worry. It was getting late – she might be worrying about him even now. He looked at Estrogard, stood up and moved quickly over to him, a little frightened.

"I want to go home," he whispered, "with you."

"Then tell them," the dragon answered softly.

So Paul explained, as politely as he could, for he didn't want to hurt their feelings, that he had spent a marvellous day with them, and that he was very very grateful for everything, especially for the rescue of his friend Estrogard, but that he already had a home and a mother and a father and a brother who would be very upset if he failed to return to them.

"Ah well," said the unicorn, "we didn't really think you would stay, but you seemed the right sort of person, so we just thought we'd try."

Then they finished their tea and made preparations for the return flight. The eagle was going to escort them most of the way "just in case" he said, and actually smiled at Paul.

They had some presents to bring back – small ones that they could manage: an ivory handled mirror for Paul's mother, a carved pipe for his father, a magnifying glass for Bill; and an ornamental basket made from a gourd for the rabbit. Paul's own gift wasn't one that had to be carried; he had three new friends, a gryphon, a unicorn and an eagle, friends he could call on at any time.

"We grow old, Paul," they explained, "but we live far longer than human beings. So we'll always be here when you want us."

They were rising slowly, Estrogard, Paul and the eagle. "Good-bye, good-bye," everyone was calling out. Paul waved happily to the royal beasts below, now small as the imprint of a king's seal.

"They're happy," murmured the boy.

# Home Again

Paul knew nothing of the journey home for he slept soundly all the way nestling between Estrogard's wings, while the eagle hovered above keeping a very protective eye on the boy and on the basket of presents that hung on the child's arm. He had not originally intended to accompany them the whole way home, but when he saw that Paul was asleep, he wanted to stay for fear the child should fall again.

So he stayed until they reached the Dragon Rock, and then accepted Estrogard's invitation to spend the night with him on the mountain. He flew back to the summit to wait, while Mr. Nogard carried the sleeping boy through the forest, down the stony path, along the street past the drowsy villagers idly chatting and smoking their pipes or gossiping over their knitting. Most of them had a friendly word for Mr. Nogard, though some stared and a few whispered.

"Scandalous. Had that boy out all day yesterday, all day again today. In the glaring sun, too. No wonder . . . the poor child . . . His mother, what she puts up with. . . . Nearly out of her mind . . . Too much freedom, these youngsters . . ."

But by this time Mr. Nogard was well out of earshot and turning in at the gate of Paul's home. His mother who had been anxiously watching at the window ran out to meet him.

"Ssh," whispered Mr. Nogard, seeing her worried face. "He's asleep that's all."

"Oh," she gasped, relieved. "Thank you. I know it's not late, but I began to be worried. He didn't say he'd be with you, though I thought he must be. Oh but . . . let me take him, you must be tired."

"No indeed," replied Mr. Nogard. "He's too big for you to be holding. Let me take him up to his bedroom. He'll sleep till tomorrow."

So it was that Mr. Nogard for the first time went into Paul's home. While his mother fussed around, taking the boy's sandals off and putting the basket of presents in a safe place, Mr. Nogard laid him gently on his bed, covered him up and tucked him in.

"Are you sure he's all right?" asked the anxious mother, for Paul had not so much as flickered an eyelid all the while.

"Quite sure – listen to his breathing." It was

deep and regular, his forehead felt cool, his pulse was normal. She smiled at Mr. Nogard and they went downstairs together.

"You'll stay for a meal, won't you?" she invited.

"That's very good of you, but I can't stay long – I have to be through the forest before nightfall."

"You're wise." said Paul's father Simon . "It doesn't do to be going through that forest in the dark."

Mary, his wife, was already clattering cups and saucers. "Pull up now to the table, all. It's ready and waiting."

Black pudding, eggs, ham, potatoes with lumps of butter, home-made bread – Mary had a fine supper prepared, and she was pleased to see Mr. Nogard enjoying it as he and Simon talked about the price of cattle at the last fair.

"It was very good of you to look after Paul all day," she said between mouthfuls. "I hope he was no trouble."

"We had a bit of excitement, but he was good."

"Well, I hope so. He can be a downright scamp when he wants."

"Ah, he's only a boy, Mary," said Simon. "He seems to like being with you, though," he continued, turning to Mr. Nogard. "I'd say you're good for him. He's a bit of a dreamer at times, and I often feel he needs a bit more scope than we can give him. In a way, you're two of a kind."

"All the same, he musn't be taking up too much of Mr. Nogard's time." Mary would not have any of her children imposing on other people.

"Oh, he's hardly had any of my time yet, and I enjoy having him," said Mr. Nogard, hastening to reassure Mary in case she might stop Paul's visits.

Mary was not entirely convinced, but there was no time for further discussion as the sun was already beginning to sink. They rose from the supper table, bade each other goodnight, and soon Mr. Nogard was striding back towards the forest, nodding a greeting at anyone he met.

"I suppose it's all right," Mary said as she watched his retreating form.

"What?"

"Paul and him."

"Why shouldn't it be?"

"I don't know. I suppose I just don't like to see my child going off with a stranger."

"But he's not a stranger, Mary. And Paul hasn't gone off with him either."

"No, you're right. There's something very nice about him really," she smiled as she remembered the way he had tucked Paul up in bed.

"He's all right," said Simon.

They walked back into their house together.

# Paul's Gift

When Paul awoke it was broad daylight. He sat up in bed feeling sticky and crumpled and rubbed his eyes, trying to remember where he ought to be. This was his own bedroom – that was a good thing. His mother was humming a gay tune downstairs – that was even better. People sometimes had strange dreams; he remembered reading stories that ended: "And I awoke and found myself in bed. It had all been a dream."

He hoped it had not all been a dream. Then he caught sight of the basket of presents. "Ah!" he smiled with satisfaction. "It wasn't."

He took the basket and ran downstairs to his mother.

"Hello love," she said happily, as he gave her a hug." "You did have a good sleep. Do you know it's nearly dinner-time? All the others have been out making hay since morning."

"Can I go too?"

"Yes, when you've had some breakfast, and put on a clean shirt. Now run off and wash – you're filthy. Wherever did you get to yesterday? Oh, and you've got blackberry juice on your shirt. Paul! You know that won't wash out! You really should be more considerate."

"I'm sorry, Mum," Paul looked ruefully at his shirt. It was in a pretty bad state. "I won't wear any shirt today."

"Oh, go off with you now." His mother laughed. Children were ridiculous.

He didn't much like washing, but the sea was just across the road, so he slipped in for a swim. This was a painless way of removing the dirt. When he returned his breakfast was on the table.

"What's in the basket, Paul?"

"A surprise. Close your eyes."

She did so and Paul drew out the mirror and held it before her.

"Now you can look."

She gave a gasp of astonishment as she saw the delicate craftsmanship of the ivory-backed mirror. "Oh Paul – where did you get that?"

"A friend of Mr. Nogard's gave it to me."

"But you shouldn't accept presents like this. It's a terribly expensive one. You'll have to give it back."

"I can't – besides they wanted me to have it and they've got lots more things. Look what they gave me for Dad and Bill. And anyway, I won't be seeing them for a long time."

"But Paul you don't understand. They're strangers. You can't take expensive gifts from strangers. Who are 'they' anyway?"

Suddenly the matter had become immensely complicated. His mother naturally assumed that 'they' were human beings, and she was not going to be under any obligation to 'them'. And yet it was all very simple if you understood about the gryphon and the unicorn.

But Paul could never hope to be believed if he talked about having lunch and tea with a pair of heraldic beasts. How could he explain matters so that she would be pacified?

"Look, Mum, you see Mr. Nogard took me to this island where an old couple live by themselves. They've got pots of money, but they were so pleased to see me that they gave me these presents to bring back."

Mary was examining the gifts minutely. "On an island? Sounds highly suspicious to me. I wouldn't be surprised if these are stolen goods – ready for the black market."

"Oh Mum! They're not! You should have seen this old couple. It all belongs to them."

"Look, Paul. I'm your mother. Now believe me, ordinary people don't have things like these to throw away unless they want to get rid of them for some reason."

"They just wanted to give me something to take

home. And we looked around for things we thought you'd like. That's all." Paul's throat was beginning to feel tight with disappointment. He knew she had never owned anything so pretty as the mirror, and had expected her to be delighted. He ate his breakfast in silence, determined not to cry.

"I'll put them on the mantlepiece and ask your father."

Paul said nothing until he was ready to go out. Then a thought struck him. "Why don't you ask Mr. Nogard?" That would be the best solution. Mr. Nogard would understand how to deal with grown-ups. You couldn't rely on them; they always got things the wrong way round.

"Yes – yes, we'll do that. Bring him home for supper. I'll be sending your dinner out to you in the field."

"Bye, mum."

"Bye now, love. Take care."

He set off at a jog-trot, feeling slightly happier; but grown-ups in general were the limit.

He could hear shouts, laughter and singing from the hay-fields, and soon he was racing across the meadow, between haystacks to where Spike and the other boys were building a large rick. He was soon among them, pitching the hay up – sometimes onto the rick, sometimes onto Spike. They were grappling with each other after one such attack, and Paul was sitting astride his flattened friend when Spike asked, "Where were you all yesterday and the day before?"

This was it. Spike was his best friend. Paul decided to tell him everything.

"I went up the mountain with Mr. Nogard – through the forest and right to the top of the mountain."

"Cor," breathed Spike. "Wish he'd taken me."

"He lives in a cave – it's beautiful – large rooms, all light, lots of food – birds and rabbits bringing him presents, talking to him. . . ."

Spike laughed a little, but thought he understood.

"But the most fantastic thing is that when we were on the way up Mr. Nogard changed into a red dragon with golden wings."

"Oh *ha ha ha*." Spike rolled over and stood up, for Paul had relaxed his hold. "You'd just got me interested. I nearly believed you. Where did you go though?"

"It's true. I went with him. He's a dragon."

"Oh yes. And I suppose you sat on his back and flew over the sea."

"I did."

"Tell that to the girls. They might believe you. You're going daft. Here everyone – come and listen to this. He thinks Mr. Nogard's a dragon."

"Oh clever dick. Just because that's what his name says backwards." A small fellow with spectacles laughed mockingly. Paul looked around at the circle of boys all eyeing him with scorn.

"Thinks he lives in fairyland, does he?"

"Mind the goblins don't run off with you!"

Paul's temper was rising. He clenched and

unclenched his fists glaring at Spike. Everyone was suddenly quiet.

"Sissy!" hissed Spike.

Then Paul lunged, arms flailing, and soon Spike and he were thrashing about, rolling, kicking, punching. The onlookers, not really interested in what had caused the fight, had taken sides and were chanting, some for Paul, some for Spike. At last, with a forceful thrust, Spike flung Paul against the side of the hayrick which began to topple. Now, what had begun as a single fight became a pitched battle, as the hay fell down upon the struggling boys, and they wrestled, half buried in a confusion of kicking legs, beating arms and hay.

The men were quick to arrive, but not quick enough to prevent the destruction of a morning's work.

"What do you think you're doing?"

"Hey there! You! Come out of that."

"Keep still now, or you'll know all about it . . ."

Strong arms dragged kicking and wrestling boys from the ruins of the demolished haystack.

"Who started it?"

Paul had opened his mouth to say "I did" when there was a general chorus

"We all did."

"Well you can all build up the haystack again. And there won't be any dinner until it's done. And if there's any more fighting I'll flay the lot of you." Paul's father was roused. "Bill, you'll have to stay with them and see it's done properly."

Bill looked decidely disgruntled at this, but just then Mr. Nogard appeared.

"Look, Simon, I'll keep an eye on them."

"That's good of you; thanks, Mr. Nogard. Then come and share dinner with us."

The men moved off to work for another few minutes before stopping for a meal. The boys looked ruefully at the devastation. But within minutes they were laughing and singing again as they tossed up the hay to Paul and Spike who straddled the rick, making it firm. It did not take too long under Mr. Nogard's direction, and at last they were able to collapse on the ground to devour mountains of potatoes and butter.

Mr. Nogard walked home with Simon that evening and again stayed to supper. It only took him a little time to reassure Mary that the presents were indeed genuine gifts.

"You've no need to worry Mary. The couple are very old friends of mine. I've known them for years. They collect antiques, trinkets and the like, but it gives them great pleasure now and again to make an unexpected present to a visitor. Believe me, if you saw the pleasure they have in giving, you'd never worry about receiving gifts from them."

"Ah, the poor old things," said Mary, visualising a tottering old gentleman with a beard, and a lady in grey silk with lace collar and cuffs. "Then it was a kindness to visit them."

"It was indeed," replied Mr. Nogard. Paul exchanged a smile with him. He knew all along that

Mr. Nogard wouldn't let him down. And that closed the discussion.

After the supper had been cleared and the dishes washed Paul walked with his friend through the village towards the forest. They had plenty of time for it was still light, so they sat down on the hillside, listening to the evening birds.

"What was the fight about Paul?"

"You," Paul said, pulling at little tufts of grass.

"I thought that might happen." Mr. Nogard puffed quietly at his pipe.

"Why doesn't anyone believe me? Why is it so difficult to make them understand?"

Mr. Nogard watched a blue smoke ring float away before he replied. "It's unusual. That's all. People aren't used to discovering that a man may be a dragon. Or that a dragon and a boy may be friends."

"If it had been Spike, and he'd told me you were a dragon . . ."

"Would you have believed him?"

"Yes, I would. It wouldn't have struck me as strange at all."

"Which goes to prove that you're the only boy in the village who could be my friend, because you're the only one prepared to believe in me."

"But if Spike had seen you as you really are . . ."

"He wouldn't have been able to. You see me because it's not only your eyes that are open – your heart is too. And that was open before we ever went up the mountain."

It was all right then. All Paul's questions had been answered. He knew now why he would never see Estrogard in the village.

"It still seems a pity I can't talk to anyone else about Estrogard."

"It is a pity in a way, but it doesn't really matter because you know and I know. You can always have a chat with the birds and rabbits. They're always ready to listen."

Paul laughed. "Yes, but they never answer – at least I don't understand what they say."

"Don't you? How did you manage with eagle, then?"

Paul sat up with a jerk. "And the unicorn, and the gryphon?" Mr. Nogard continued.

"Oh . . . oh . . . but weren't they different?"

"Why should they have been?"

The boy's eyes were wide with astonishment. "Was it you? Did you make me able to understand?"

Mr. Nogard smiled again. A thrush pierced the laughing stillness. "Estrogard and Paul," she sang, "are friends."

# Part Two

# A Spark of Fire

Five summers of adventure and winters of memories had passed since Paul had first visited the dragon's lair, and every autumn Estrogard would begin to feel sad, for he knew it was time to think of flying East to see the other dragons. He had to call on them all as far as he could – he felt a certain brotherly responsibility for them. Living alone as they did, dragons had all kinds of needs; some were quite helpless and Estrogard knew that if he didn't pay attention to them, nobody else would. Still, he hated leaving his home and always stayed until the very last minute, making especially sure that the little sunbeam was asleep for the winter before he left.

He had arranged with Paul that a dove would carry messages between them; then the winter would not seem so long. It was a good arrangement in the circumstances, and worked very well. Now it was nearly winter again, and time for Estrogard to make his long journey to the east. They discussed it seriously, stretched out in the September sunshine – as seriously as you can when rabbits keep hopping over you.

"This is going to be the most important journey I've ever made," said Estrogard. There is to be a conference of all the dragons from the whole earth, sea and sky, on a mountain specially constructed for the occasion on an island near the great empire of the East." He chuckled. "There's been a select committee to arrange accommodation for the earth dragons, water dragons and sky dragons. I made a few enemies last time I was over there – somebody nominated me for the committee instead of old Fuhalla. I was only too glad to stand down – it would have meant being away from the village for two whole years, and I didn't fancy that. I withdrew in his favour, but all the same, he didn't like it."

"We'd have missed you."

"Yes, well, I must admit there's more of my heart here than on an island in the East with a band of squabbling brother dragons."

"Do they all squabble?"

"Oh no, not at all. Only the type that get themselves elected onto accommodation committees. I don't see what all the fuss is, anyway. I'd be quite happy to doss down under a cosy boulder for a week; but some of them are very conscious of their dignity, and want a freshly hewn cave or clean river bed all to themselves. I suppose for some of them, dignity is all they have – they didn't all find a friend as I did."

He smiled at Paul, and they were silent for a little while, enjoying the warmth of the sun. A young rabbit popped his head out of the earth between them, then scampered away as Paul made a grab for the little white cotton-tail.

"I miss all this in the winter time," said Paul, "the rabbits, the rainbow, the little sunbeam – and you."

"Yes, me too. But we have to do our work."

"Still, you know, it isn't all that lonely," continued the boy. "Sometimes when I'm with the others and we're laughing and enjoying ourselves, I have the feeling that you're there too, and that's why we're having such a good time. Everyone says that the best times of the summer are always with you. And then, when I see the flames flickering in the grate, it sometimes seems as if a spark of your fire has got inside me, and is dancing with the other fire. And then I laugh, and my father thinks I'm crazy."

"You have got a spark of my fire inside you," said the dragon, "and what's more, I have a spark of yours."

"Of mine?"

"Of course."

"Where did I get fire from? I'm no dragon."

"Everyone has fire, but they don't all give it a

chance. Fire needs air and room to spread. If you set it free it will dance and make people happy with its warmth, and when it meets another fire it will leap up and join in, and fill the place with light and heat. But some stifle their fires altogether; others have smouldering embers, and if they don't open in time they soon have only ashes. But you have a fire within you that is worthy of a dragon. It is splendid and free, and it leapt up to greet me just when my flame was beginning to give up hope of ever finding another spark to join with."

Paul was silent in wonderment. "Are you talking about me?" he said at last.

"I'm talking about us."

"How did you find my fire?"

"It was shining in your eyes."

Then he understood. On the mountain, in the palace, the dragon's eyes had always soothed his fears and filled him with unutterable joy. And this was the reason: together they had kindled new fire.

After a profound silence, Paul spoke again. "Why did you say this was going to be the most important journey of your life?"

"Because I shall tell all my brother dragons that I have found the key that every dragon seeks but few find. I shall hold it out to them, and maybe some will accept it, but I fear many will reject it."

"What's it the key to?"

"The kingdom of true happiness."

"And you've found it?"

"Yes, I've found it. I found it on an evening

when a boy laughed with me, and a thrush sang – quite a long time ago."

Again Paul was struck dumb with wonder. How well he remembered the evening! And how amazing that the key to Estrogard's wonderful kingdom should have been found with him. It seemed an incredible mystery.

"I shall tell all my brother dragons, I shall shout it to the four winds: the key to the kingdom of true happiness is love."

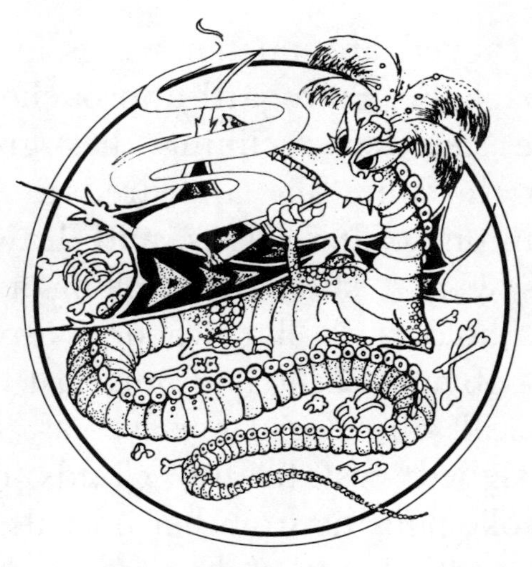

# Wilhella

By the time the mountain was covered with snow, Estrogard was well on his way to the great empire. He had to call at many places: the land of the midnight sun, the golden deserts, the cold oceans where ice throws a green glow on everything; the brilliant tropics where rainbow-fish dart through clear blue water. All the realms of light he visited. Anywhere there was a dragon he stopped, too, to pay his respects and make sure the dragon knew of the Great Assembly in the East.

He met one lady dragon on a small, private island in the Pacific. In her youth she must have been exceptionally beautiful, for even now, in her second century, she had a tarnished attractiveness. The scales of her body, tipped with gold, still had a dull gleam, but her age was betrayed by the folds of skin which sagged around her wings and wrinkled along her back. As Estrogard approached her from the sky, he saw her reclining, her green length uncoiled in the sun. She appeared to be holding something in one of her talons, and drawing closer, Estrogard saw that she was smoking a cigar in a long, silver holder. A flat wooden box lay open beside her – obviously she had only just begun for it was almost full. She closed her eyes as she inhaled, and then sighed ecstatically, clouds of strongly smelling smoke pouring from her nostrils.

She was startled out of her trance by a warm greeting; she had not been expecting another visitor so soon, but her cunning mind knew that she must not look surprised. Languidly she opened one sloe-black eye, and closed it, looking bored, but in reality being more surprised than ever. A slight tremor passed through her body betraying the emotion she felt. Estrogard had called in.

"Hmm – long time no see." Wilhella felt a little snappy – angry at having been taken unawares, the stickiness of sleep still upon her.

"That's a bright welcome," said Estrogard sarcastically. "I didn't know you smoked," he added, to fill a gap.

"I've only just taken it up," replied Wilhella.

"They say it's bad for the lungs."

This wasn't much of a conversation.

"Do you have to start an argument every time you come?" demanded the lady. Her snappiness was not going to pass. "It's only bad for human lungs. How could a dragon be affected by cigar smoke? Every time you come over here you say something dumber than the last time."

"What was it last time?"

"Oh how can I remember? You're always telling me what to do and none of it ever applies. You think you know better than any other dragon in the whole wide universe. I never knew anyone so conceited!"

"Sorry, Wilhella. If I'd known I was disturbing your siesta I'd have dropped by on my way back."

"Don't try to put the blame on my siesta. It's you. You're always insulting my intelligence."

This conversation was getting nowhere. Estrogard decided to move on.

"I was just calling in to let you know about the Great Assembly. I'm going to it."

Now Wilhella sat up and looked really angry.

"Who arranged it all?" she demanded. "That's just like you, isn't it, you great know-all? You have these enormous secrets and you have to keep them to yourself so that you get there first and have the best cave and all the attention. And I suppose you think you'll talk to all the elders and dine on the high table and have everyone bowing and scraping to you while I'm . . ."

"Wait a minute, Wilhella. Calm down. I called in for a friendly chat and to tell you that you'll get a great welcome if you come; and all you do is shout at me."

"I don't think I want to come," replied Wilhella

huffily, but not quite so crossly. "I don't like going on my own to places; you know that."

Estrograd laughed to himself at this ridiculous statement; but soon he had persuaded her to fly with him to the East, where they would arrive together and in time for all the festivities as well as the hard work. Somewhat mollified, she invited him into her cave for a meal, and, to show that there was no more ill feeling, she even gave him a cigar.

It was hard to find a smooth place to sit down; the floor of Wilhella's cave was strewn with bones, some whitened, some charred, all reeking more or less with the same stench, difficult to identify, but revolting enough. Estrograd's tail swept a space clear and he squatted amid the fragments of ancient meals, natural dust and tobacco ash, which rose in little clouds as he moved, and settled in a thin film on his red and gold body once he was still.

"Had many visitors lately?" he asked.

Wilhella smiled wickedly to herself.

"Plenty," was her cryptic reply.

"Nice?"

"Various." Again her expression was smug but she was giving nothing away.

"I just wondered," began Estrogard, whose suspicions were being rapidly confirmed. "Do you find they like coming here?"

At this, Wilhella threw back her head and laughed harshly.

"Like it?" she cried. "You can't hold them back when they meet me – and they never ask to go home. I treat them all the same, you see, whether they suit me or not . . ." Her sentence trailed off into a wicked chuckle.

"All right, Wilhella, show me how you do it. What's your trick this time?" She shrieked joyously, "Oho, I've got you now! You hoped I'd reform, didn't you? No, no, my boy – I've too many tricks left yet. If you want to know how I catch them, I'll tell you – it's my voice."

"Your – voice?"

"Yes, my voice," she said, dropping into a deep, husky tone. She closed her eyes and crooned softly. Estrogard smiled in spite of himself. She was good at it.

"And when those poor devils see me – oh boy – we have a party and singing and dancing, and they bring me cigars and I make them laugh and feed them up nice and fat and they forget all their troubles. And then," she went on innocently, "I think of my old friend, Estrogard. He always said 'Make people happy and they'll make you happy too'. So when they're sleeping sweetly I go round softly, so as not to disturb them, and have a real juicy meal of each one. And they never wake up to this old world of sorrow any more. So they're happy. And I've had a – mmm – scrumptious feast, so I'm happy. Oh, I'm a good girl now." Her expression hardened and her black eyes grew small. "So I win this round, boyo, *I* win."

"Yes, Wilhella," said Estrogard, a little bitterly. "You win. You're yourself, you'll never change.

Keep making yourself happy."

"Now don't you start insulting me again. Keep your nose out of my business. I'm a real dragon, not a wet sop like you. I've got fire in my guts and murder on my claws. What can you do? Nothing but go around upsetting decent dragons with your drivel about kindness and love. Why don't you go and rip up a few children? Then you'd know what it feels like to have strength – then you'd be real . . ."

She could not finish her sentence. Estrogard had risen and with a rapid movement quicker than sight had slipped beneath Wilhella's cumbersome frame and was now spinning round in lightning coils, Wilhella pinioned on his back by his two powerful wings, gasping and spluttering in anger and shame at the indignity. He was playing with her like a baby, and, fastened as she was, she was utterly powerless to speak or move. The trick only lasted a few seconds. Estrogard carried her outside the cave and released her, then quickly mounted into the air.

She was sobbing with fury, belching fire and black smoke, but it could not reach him. For a long time as he flew into the distance he could hear screeching after him. "Just you wait, I'm coming to the Great Assembly. You'll pay for this. You haven't heard the last of it yet. You can't treat me like that. You'll pay for it. Just you wait!"

# The Great Assembly

Estrogard was greetly warmly by his fellow dragons when he reached the island. Fuhalla was among the first to welcome him, and bustled up officiously, to hope Estrograd would find his accommodation to his liking.

"Oh, anything will do me," said Estrogard.

"Not at all, not at all," replied Fuhalla, his tail writhing fulsomely. "But come, let me show you." He shuffled off at a rapid pace, having no wings, but hooves instead of talons, and not to make him feel inferior, Estrogard slithered along the uphill path.

Certainly the accommodation committee had done their planning very well. Several artificial streams ran parallel down the mountainside, periodically ending in pools so that the water dragons might feel at home. Multi-storey caves honeycombed the slopes, and fountains from just below the summit provided permanent evaporation, so that clouds would form for the few who could only sleep in the air. There was still plenty of room for exercise – some dragons are several metres long, so they require ample circulation space. There were free expanses of grass, rock, newly hewn boulders for sunbathing and clear strips for landing and taking off. Estrogard congratulated Fuhalla on the geometrical precision of the planning.

"Yes, yes, it's all mathematics now. None of your old breathe and blast methods. I mean, a century ago you'd never know whether you were blowing out a cave two yards or two miles deep. Yes, I've got plans for modernising all dragon's lairs. Clean sharp lines. None of those unexpected nooks and corners where you might split your skull on an overhanging piece of rock. I'm hoping to get a permit to go on a tour of inspection and renovation."

Estrograd thought of his home with the quartz slab and the opal chute, the spider's web ceiling and the rainbow arch. He thought of the little sunbeam, and the games they all had played just because there were so many unexpected nooks and corners. Fuhalla's voice was going like ticker tape. He imagined him turning out the room where the nightingale spun her song, and the happy laughter of Paul and Mr. Nogard still made the thrush sing. He shivered.

"You cold?" asked Fuhalla sharply. He didn't

miss a thing.

"Not at all. Just a little tired." Estrogard excused himself, and suddenly became aware of a need to keep a guard over his reactions. Fuhalla, for all his affability, was watching him. He could see no reason for it, but instinctively he felt that he would have to be careful.

They were near the summit now, and Fuhalla stopped. A single ring of caves ran round the mountain here, each one self-contained, larger, more secluded than those lower down.

"This one is yours, Estrogard, my old friend; number A4."

Estrogard looked at him with a query in his eyes.

"We are old friends, aren't we, eh? Something seems to be troubling you."

"I'm wondering why you have placed me up here and not down among the others." As he said this he was looking towards the honeycomb of caves and could see dragons of all colours streaming into them, apparently without guides, for there seemed to be much jostling and pushing to reach the upper caves which were the most popular, presumably because they had the best view.

"Aha!" Fuhalla laughed meaningfully. "Lordly house for the lordly." Without further explanation, but with a strange gleam in his eye, Fuhalla waddled away and was soon slithering down the smooth path. Estrogard stared after him, and long after the sound of his rough hide had ceased to grate on the rock, he was still pondering his final words and trying to decide whether the gleam in his eye was malicious or merely secretive.

He felt strangely disturbed, and climbed a few yards to the top of the mountain to look out over the sea. The sun was beginning to sink in the West, far away over his land, his own mountain, his home. Somewhere out there were people with hearts. The dragons, so far, had not impressed him much. He shrugged the thought away. It was ridiculous to judge all dragons on the two he had encountered. He knew there were plenty of different ones. He'd meet them tomorrow.

He sighed as he gazed out to sea. The sooner the Great Assembly was over, the better. He'd make for home straight away, and arrive just at the beginning of spring. He closed his eyes to see the daffodils and crocuses already, and was smiling when a gentle cooing close beside him made him look up. The dove, Paul's messenger, was here.

# Messenger from Home

She was a marvellous messenger, for she loved news and was always visiting people, exchanging titbits of information, and keeping up-to-date with the latest gossip. Excited beyond words, Estrogard took her to his cave and happily warmed some potent dragon brew that was only used on the most special occasions. You only need a few sips of it to make you feel blissfully happy, and he knew the dove would take to it without persuasion. While he busied himself with preparations for a little celebration party, (the accommodation committee had left in some provisions) she chatted away incessantly. At another time he might have felt a little irritated, for she hardly paused for breath, and if he had wanted to say anything, there would have been no gap for him to slip even half a word in. But as it was he felt he could have listened to her all night and all day, for she was bringing him news of home.

"And Jacob Dooley, his missus chasing him all round the market place with a frying pan one night in the snow, and Miss Leghorn was watching it all behind her lace curtains, and so she didn't hear someone come in her back door, and suddenly a man in black switched off all the lights and put his arms round her and gave her a smacking kiss. She had to stay in bed for a week with shock."

Estrogard was chuckling as he thought of neat little Miss Leghorn, her lips set pursed in permanent disapproval. It would do her good to be kissed. The visitor should have left the lights on.

So she went through the whole village, hopping from house to house, reproducing the conversations over garden walls, leaning on gates, sitting round cosy log fires. Though he had never been in the village in winter time. Estrogard would imagine everything and everyone as she spoke.

She had news too, of the animals on the mountain, and of the trees in the forest. "There were some trees cut down just before I left." Estrogard suddenly thought of the knotted oak that seemed sometimes to speak. "Not the ancient oak at the mouth of the forest?" he said anxiously.

"Oh no; some younger slender ones, to make telegraph poles." He felt a little sad all the same. It was a shame that proud young trees should be uprooted and made to stand branchless, looking foolish by the roadside.

They talked long into the night, undisturbed, surprisingly, by any callers.

When the dove began to run out of things to say, Estrogard would ask about so-and-so, or such a place, and she would launch out into another long and gossipy account.

"And how's my friend?" he asked at length.

"Do you mean Paul?"

"Who else?"

"He's growing," she said. "He'll be a tall young man when you get back."

"Everything all right with him?"

"Oh yes. He's getting very good-looking. The girls are all suddenly beginning to notice him."

This was a new departure. He knew that Paul would have to grow up and now he felt curious to see whether it would change him. He doubted it. There would be differences; he would have new interests, make new friends, but basically he would still be the same. At least Estrogard hoped so. He couldn't imagine Paul suddenly becoming blind to starlight, deaf to the nightingale. When he left him the flame had been burning brightly. It was unlikely that Paul would let the fire die away.

"Did he send any message for me?"

"Yes. Now what was it exactly?" He said something about a spark – I didn't really understand but he said you would. Let me see now. I think he said 'Tell Estrogard that a spark of our fire had lit another flame.' Something like that, anyway. And that he had found someone who he thought would be able to see you as you really are."

"That's good news," said Estrogard. "Who do you think he means?"

"Oh I wouldn't like to say. He's with so many people I couldn't pin it down to anyone in particular."

That was a pity. She knew so much about the village, and yet couldn't tell him the very thing he wanted to know. Still the details weren't all that important. The message was a very good one. Now he was twice as anxious to be finished with the assembly and go home, but there were four whole weeks of it, and a dragon's week is measured from moon to moon. He would have to be content with whatever news the dove chose to bring him, and hope that she would bring back reliable word from him to Paul.

He gave her a soft cushion of straw to sleep on and invited her to stay for a few days.

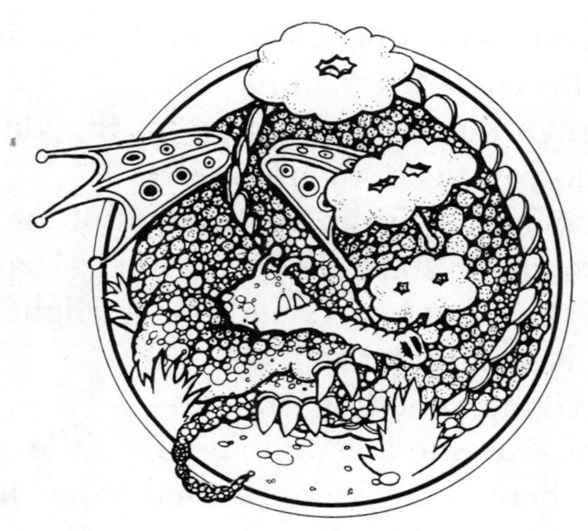

# Introducing Max

The first week of the Great Assembly was to be given over to games. This was acknowledged by all leading dragons to be an excellent way of getting to know one another, and very necessary, since dragons live, for the most part, alone. Not all were as fond of travelling and visiting as Estrogard, and indeed, many were hampered by not having wings, so there was an air of muted excitement on the first morning as they exchanged small talk, waiting for the organisers of the games to appear.

"How did you find your cave last night?"

"Passable, passable. Difficult to get used to a strange rock, though. Didn't sleep much."

"Oh – how much do you usually sleep?"

"Sundown to sunrise."

"Every night?" The enquirer was an athletic

young dragon, who opened a purple eye in wide surprise at his corpulent companion.

"Every night, and sometimes in the day, too. How long do you sleep, then?"

"That depends. I live at the bottom of the ocean, and if the moon or stars are out I don't sleep at all, I play with the moonbeams and the starlight. I only sleep when it's quite dark."

"You're young. You'll learn."

Estrogard was moving among the little groups, chatting to them. They were pleased to see him, for of all the dragons there, he was one of the few that everyone knew, on account of his annual visits.

"Quite a promising young fellow, that," remarked Max, the corpulent dragon, when Estrogard had greeted him and passed on.

"Young?" exclaimed the athletic youngster. "He's lived for centuries."

"Perhaps he has, but you ought to know, me boy, that dragons don't measure age in years, they measure it by the things they do. I've not lived as long as he has, but all I can do now is to bask in the sun, so you see I'm an old dragon. But a happy one."

With that, Max curled up to go to sleep. After all, he had been up since before sunrise, disturbed by the unfamiliar bustle of dragons performing their early morning observances. It had been very upsetting. It was all very well if you were on an island or a mountain by yourself. Then you could sing a greeting to the sun. You could stamp around your mountain doing your flexibility exercises. You could suck in gallons of water and then spray it out in a fountain over the rocks and plants if you wanted to clear out your throat. But really, to have all this and more and happen in such a confined space – he himself had received the full benefit of his next-door neighbour's spray carried in on a sudden breeze, drenching his slumbers. He hoped someone would do something about it.

Piscator, the young dragon, moved off hoping to find more active comapny. He saw Estrogard in the distance, moving with ease among the crowds, and felt slightly irritated. He hoped he would be drawn against him in some of the contests; he longed unaccountably, for the pleasure of beating him at something.

At last a tremendous gong sounded, and dragons came streaming from all sides, converging on a grassy arena, where four leading dragons stood on a platform ready to welcome them and open the Great Assembly.

The sun was hot and the speeches dragged. Picastor's irritation increased; Max, who had fallen fast asleep, conveniently on the fringe of the arena, snored loudly, little puffs of white smoke floating upwards from his nostrils.

Eventually the speakers stopped, the organisers took over and the games were ready to begin. Spectators ranged themselves in a large circle on a raised bank to survey the competitors who stood in four columns for a preliminary display of basic skills. One by one they leapt into the air turning complete somersaults without the help of wings, and performing other acrobatics. This was not competitive, and there was much good-natured laughter as some elderly dragons discovered that they were not so lithe as they once had been. After a few attempts, many of these retired gracefully, leaving the display to their more nimble brethren. When the exhibition was over, it was evident that there would be some keen competition, and all were looking forward to spectacular events from the fifty or so brilliantly coloured and versatile competitors. These would begin on the second day when the heats for fire-throwing, boulder-leaping and other field events would start.

Resting after the exertions of the display, Estrogard found himself beside Max who had been awakened by the movement of the crowd at the end of the speeches, and so had observed the whole display. He had been particularly struck by Estrogard's performance; some people might feel it unfair that one dragon should be so good at everything, but Max bore him no grudge. He realised that skill like Estrogard's was in great measure a result of constant training in keeping fit; and as Max's principal activity was sun-soaking it never occurred to him to feel jealous of anyone else who was more active. He was not stupid, however, and had noticed with interest the way Piscator was watching Estrogard throughout the display and quite evidently trying to outdo him.

"You shouldn't be so good at everything, you know," he said to Estrogard, as they lay drowsily in the afternoon sun. Estrogard laughed. "Others are as good as me."

"Unfortunately, no," replied Max. After a long pause for rumination, Max continued, "Unless you let them be."

"What do you mean?" asked Estrogard in surprise.

"I mean that it might be a better thing for you if you were to allow yourself to be beaten in some of the games."

For a while, Estrogard was silent, astonished. He tried to imagine what Max could be driving at. He waited for him to speak again, knowing that he always took a long time to work out an idea fully, but that it would be worth hearing eventually.

"I was watching."

"Yes?" said Estrogard expectantly; but nothing else was forthcoming for the time being. Estrogard thought Max had fallen asleep, and he had just become resigned to a long wait, when Max completed the sentence:

"And I could see that you would win every single game."

"That's ridiculous," replied Estrogard. "There are a number of games I haven't even entered for."

"Even so, you're going to be the winner."

"Well, I don't see why that should be such a disaster."

"No, I know you don't. That's just the trouble.

You know a lot, Estrogard. Far more than I do, but this is your blind spot."

It sounded like a riddle. Estrogard would simply have to be patient and wait for Max to explain; he was being unusually pessimistic, and this alone made Estrogard take him seriously.

"If you win the games, I'm sorry for you."

"But Max, I'm not competing just to win. I'm doing it because I enjoy it, and if I should happen to be the best, then why shouldn't I have the glory?"

"You see? I told you. Blind."

Estrogard sighed. Well – there was all afternoon. He could wait.

"What would you feel if one of those young squirts won the games?"

"I expect they will – I'll be delighted."

Max looked at him closely. "He means it, too! That's what makes you so blind. You mark my words Estrogard; everybody isn't like you. Some of these dragons want very badly to win. And I'm not sure, but I have a funny feeling that some of them want you to lose."

The slightly nagging anxiety that Estrogard had experienced on the previous day with Fuhalla now returned as Max's words sank in. And yet there could be no reason for hostility: he himself had far more friends among the assembled dragons than any other there. Besides he really wanted to compete and try his strength against dragons much younger than himself; he enjoyed the feeling of soaring above everyone else. At any rate, it would be impossible for him to try not to win. If he were going to take part at all, he would have to do his best – otherwise he might as well become a spectator.

"Do you think I ought not to compete at all?"

"You can't back out now – no one would let you."

"Then I can't purposely try to lose."

Max did not reply. He had known this would be the out-come, and yet he felt he had to try and warn Estrogard, at least. He hoped he was only being cynical, but he had had so much leisure time to observe and think that he was a very good judge of a situation, and thought he could see the way this one would work out.

"You know, Estrogard, you're a very fine example of dragonhood, but you've one fault."

"What's that, philosopher?" Estrogard was amused.

"You always want to excel. That can be a good thing; but be careful. It may be your ruination."

Estrogard was very pensive that evening. There was truth in what Max had said, and yet he could not bring himself to act any differently. Dragons! How complicated life could be when they lived together. He consoled himself by giving a long message to the dove and sending her off. The sooner she left, the sooner he would have a reply.

# Jealousy

As the games progressed, the vague anxiety which Max had stirred in Estrogard died away. On the first day, it is true, he had begun to think there might be something in his warning, for he had won the heats with ease. However, he was not always successful after that, and had noticed a very young dragon – Piscator, he heard them call him – who had been doing very well. All the same, he realised that he would be competing in a number of final events, and was certainly well in the running for the championship.

Max kept quiet, but he was watching. He was watching the competitors and he was watching the spectators, and what he saw made him uneasy. Often he passed little groups talking in undertones, and it did not take him long to notice that Wilhella would always be in the centre of such a group.

She had arrived a few days late, making a spectacular entry as she swooped from the air in a flurry of green and bronze, and landed in the centre of the arena just at the end of one of the morning's sessions. Immediately she was surrounded by swarms of attentive dragons, jostling each other, eager to welcome her. Estrogard, she noticed, was not among them. Well – she tossed her head slightly – he would be sorry.

Max had become a byword among the dragons by this time, for wanting to sleep, and so they took no notice of him when he lay coiled on the fringe of their little groups. Gradually he learned that Wilhella had, for some reason, a strong feeling of resentment against Estrogard, and that she was subtly, insidiously, poisoning the minds of other dragons against him. It had not taken her long to discover that Fuhalla, too, bore him a grudge, and very quickly she had worked on him. She felt so helpless among all these virile male dragons, she said. It was so comforting to have someone strong and protective like Fuhalla to look after you. He wouldn't ever, ever leave her alone, would he? Because she just wouldn't know how to manage. Fuhalla straightened his tail, flexed his rather ancient muscles, and assured her that he would be her devoted escort. Together they went among the spectator dragons, talking of Estrogard, saying that of course was quite clear to see that all he wanted was to get to the top and rule over them all. Here he was, doing his best to put everyone else out of the running for the championship – couldn't they see that with their own eyes? Some dragons who had been knocked out of the games and felt annoyed, agreed; it was hard to disagree when Estrogard was actually doing so well in front of them. Others who admired and enjoyed watching him disagreed. "I can't believe it's true, Fuhalla; he's simply the best one here. And anyway, don't I remember that he gave up the job on the accommodation committee to you, though all the leaders had elected him?"

"Policy, policy," replied Fuhalla. "He's much cleverer than you or me. He did that just to put people off the scent, so that they'd think he couldn't possibly want power. And he obviously succeeded with you, my friend. So all I can do is warn you to look carefully and judge for yourself."

"I can't see that it would be such a bad thing if Estrogard did eventually become one of the leaders." Another dragon was speaking. "We all know him, and every one of use has some cause to be grateful to him. He had done many a kindness on his winter visits. He seems to me just the right type to become a leader."

"Ah, but don't you see what has been happening?" Fuhalla's voice was oily. "He has spent years – centuries – leading up to this. Estrogard's no fool. He knows how to win popularity. Make yourself known, move among the ordinary folk, do things to make them feel obliged to you – oh, it's an old, old recipe. Then, when you have them where you want them, prove by some spectacular show that you are superior in every way, and it's done. 'Why not?' you may ask. Why not indeed? Why not give power to someone who can plan and calculate and control your life without your even realising it? Why not let him take over completely? I can see that every dragon here would lie at his feet and be glad to die for him. Oh yes, Estrogard has been very, very clever. He has the whole assembly in such a state that he only needs to flick his tail and his slightest wish is granted. If that's the way you want it, then there's nothing more for me to do. I only spoke because I can see the sort of thing that's going to happen to everyone of you. And poor Wilhella can tell you about that."

This was Wilhella's cue, for a delicate little sniff, as a well-timed tear rolled down her cheek. "I'm sorry to be so stupid. Please excuse me. But once I . . . I loved Estrogard. I still love him." Pause for a slight sob, and a second tear followed the first. "But for your sakes I must forget all I ever felt for him, and tell you that your lives are in danger. Estrogard has no scruples. He'll use you, then when he's finished he'll betray you, drop you, abandon you. He left me alone on an island, young, inexperienced, defenceless . . ."

Again she broke off, apparently too moved to continue. Max was interested – a good little actress, he thought. She spoiled the show, though, by looking up to see how her audience were taking it.

But only Max noticed that; the others were too engrossed in their own thoughts, trying to assess what they had just heard. Some were completely won over to Wilhella's party. Others were not – they would observe and see for themselves. Ambition was indeed a terrible thing, and must be stamped out at all costs, but Estrogard must be proved guilty before any action could be taken.

Max was genuinely worried. It seemed to him that although Estrogard was well-loved, there was no one willing to do as much for him as the Fuhalla-Wilhella team was doing against him. Dragons listened, disagreed, observed and waited, but not one of them thought of doing anything. Perhaps they felt that Estrogard could take care of himself; he was, after all, always in control of things.

Estrogard noticed none of this. When he passed the spectators, flushed from his exertions, he did not notice that fewer and fewer came to congratulate him. There were still enough surrounding him of those who wanted to keep on the right side, just in case he did one day become the greatest leader. And there were some genuine friends who enjoyed his company, and laughed and joked with him.

It occurred to Max with some feeling of surprise, that if Estrogard were to be protected, *he* would have to take action. Action! What action could such an idle fellow as Max take? There was only one course open to him, and that was to follow Wilhella's example by quietly influencing other dragons' opinions. He had already observed several who had stood out against her evil whispering, and there were still members that had not been reached by her as yet. Would it be better to start with these, or with the ones who had resisted? The latter might be irritated by a second attempt to sway their views, and might turn against Estrogard just because they were annoyed with Max. It would be better to break fresh ground.

He laughed ruefully at himself. Here was old Max, about to become the spearhead of an underground resistance movement; Max who had never done anything more active than catch a few fish to eat, and had only come to the Great Assembly because it gave him an excuse to miss the winter at home, and come to a climate of permanent sun. Funny how you got caught up in things before you knew where you were.

His approach was less wily than Wilhella's, but shrewd. It was easy for him to assess the type of characters he was dealing with, for he would get a group engaged in conversation, then pretend to fall asleep and see how they reacted towards him. If they mocked him or made rude comments when they thought he was asleep, he knew they were no use to him. But if they laughed good-naturedly, and then continued their discussion, he felt that these might well be the ones who would be honest enough to support Estrogard. He would make it his business, then, to meet these privately and explain quite openly about the enemies of Estrogard. He would state simply what he believed of Estrogard, and ask for their suport if there should be a crisis. Many of them thought at first that here was old Max going funny in the head; when they were later tackled by Fuhalla, they began to treat him with more respect.

And Estrogard continued vaulting, swooping, somersaulting, unaware that the assembly was rapidly being split into three – for him, against him and neutral.

Max had come for the sun – he had not expected to find himself in the centre of such seething heat.

# The Dragon Games

There were now only two days left of the games. On the first, the finals would be played out. On the second and last, everyone would celebrate the champion. It was quite clear to all that there were really only two candidates for the championship; although other dragons would be taking part, all eyes were on Piscator and Estrogard.

The atmosphere was tense as the games began that morning: everyone except, apparently, Estrogard and a few of the leading dragons seemed to realise that more than a mere athletic championship was at stake. If Estrogard won, it would give Fuhalla and Wilhella an opportunity of reinforcing their statements that Estrogard was only seeking power. Some of the neutrals might become anxious and turn against him when they saw him wearing the victor's golden crown. If Piscator won, Estrogard would undoubtedly lose face both before his opponents and his supporters who would feel cheated and angry if Estrogard did not prove himself to be the best. Max did not know what to hope for; either alternative seemed equally bad. He could only wait and watch.

The competitors were in marvellous form and performed amazing feats. One blue dragon flew around the arena setting fire to ten torches spaced at intervals and then extinguised them in one mighty breath – and all within the space of time it took for another dragon to walk ten paces. Other dragons won various contests, and the crowd gave them applause, but the loudest cheers and groans, and the most breathless silences came when Piscator or Estrogard was in the field.

By the end of the morning the two favourites were equal. Each had won five contests; no one else had more than one. The decisive encounter between the two of them would come in the afternoon.

Max noticed, with real surprise, that as the crowds dispersed for a break Piscator made straight for Wilhella and Fuhalla. It was an obvious liaison; he was only surprised that he had not observed it before. Estrogard came across to him and together they moved up the mountain toward Estrogard's cave.

"Well Max, perhaps you were more right than I thought you were. How do you feel about my chances of winning?"

"I think they're fifty-fifty."

"No – that's not what I meant. How do you *feel*? Are you still convinced that it'll do me harm?"

"Can you see any reason for that yourself?"

"No, none at all. I know that there are some who hate me, but I think maybe they've always hated me. On the other hand I've met numbers of dragons who seem only too anxious to be friendly."

Max could guess which ones they were – the creeps!

"And does that make you feel more secure?"

"I never felt insecure in the first place but at least I haven't discovered any grounds to be worried."

"Then you're all right." Max felt that there was nothing else that he could say, What was the point now just before the final contest in showing Estrogard the full picture? Better to let him act as if everything were as it had always been. Fate could take its course – Max would not interfere.

The excitement back in the arena made Max feel sick and dizzy. It was not a good atmosphere for it was made of rivalry, jealousy and hatred.

Even Estrogard's supporters were thinking mainly of themselves and hoping he would win so that they could share his glory. Max wanted to escape from it all; once he would have simply curled up and gone to sleep but life was not so easy now; he had to see Estrogard through to the end.

They had begun: fire-throwing. Piscator sent a rippling streamer of flame that sped like a burning arrow until it grew faint, then fell and went out.

The distance was marked by one of the field organisers. Then Estrogard drew himself up and hurled a ball of fire; it hurtled through the air in a slight arch and landed intact, singeing the grass before it extinguised itself. There was the length of a small dragon between the two points and a roar went up from the crowd. One to Estrogard.

Next came boulder hopping, six fairly large boulders were placed at intervals of two medium sized dragons lengths. This was both a race and a test of skill, for it was difficult to keep a balance as you leaped from one boulder to another, and still more difficult, if you were a fairly large dragon, to take off from such a small point, once you had landed. The starter blew on his silver trumpet and they were off. Estrogard had the advantage of strength but Piscator was smaller, and therefore more nimble.

Evenly balanced, they were neck and neck until Estrogard slipped on his fifth boulder, touched the ground with one talon and was disqualified. Piscator reached the finishing line without incident and was greeted by another mighty roar. One all!

Now followed a series of acrobatics that were the greatest test of skill. They were to be judged on points, awarded by the four leading dragons who were the only impartial members of the entire assembly. This was not only competition, but also display, and the dragons worked to an accompaniment of drum rolls and fanfares. At the first fanfare they sprang into action and simultaneously each formed a circle with his body and began to spin like a catherine wheel. They made four complete revolutions, then opened their wings, straightened their bodies and floated gracefully to the ground. The crowd went wild. They had never seen anything like this before. For just a moment hostility was forgotten in the genuine admiration everyone felt for two highly accomplished performers. Then the marks were announced: Estrogard six, Piscator six.

When the uproar had died down, there was a second fanfare. This time each had to hold himself rigid in a vertical line and hover a small distance above the ground – a far less spectacular, but more difficult feat. The drums rolled and they rose in the air, using their wings until they were in position, the tips of their tails about a talon's span above the grass. Then they folded their wings and hung motionless. The crowd was hushed and still as they watched – then a slight groan went up: Estrogard, too heavy to hold his position any longer, was bending slightly, and in a moment had opened his wings and come to the ground. Piscator followed only a split second later, but it was long enough to gain him extra points. Estrogard six, Piscator eight.

The third and final test was the most breathtaking of all. The fanfares blared, the drums rolled and suddenly Piscator and Estrogard had become figures of eight spinning dizzily in the sky, shooting off sparks, flashing bright rays as the sun caught the gold on their bodies. Round and round they spun, changing direction twice, until it seemed as if they were dragons no longer, but only brilliant spinning shapes. Then at last they unfolded their wings, uncoiled and flew round the arena to deafening cheers. There was little to choose between them. Piscator had, it is true, not been able to form a perfect figure at first, but this had been quickly rectified, and his movements had been every bit as controlled as Estrogard's. Nevertheless it cost him points: Piscator six, Estrogard eight – overall a dead heat.

Estrogard felt disappointed. He had hoped that these displays would have proved decisive, for they would have been an excellent way to end the contest. Now they would have to resort to a test of strength in a formal wrestling match, which would continue until one of them was pinned down beneath the other. It was the one sport he detested, for, in spite of its strict rules, it could be dangerous. He wondered how young Piscator felt. They could have a few moments' rest if they wanted – perhaps he would like just to talk for a little, and ease the tension.

They were standing together in the centre of the arena, and now Estrogard turned to face his young opponent. What he saw made him forget his desire to chat, and he moved a step backwards, recoiling from the open hatred that burned in the younger dragon's eyes. Then compassion flooded his heart; he understood at last how much it meant to Piscator that he should win these games. The poor youngster had set his heart on the golden crown.

How useless that was, yet what happiness it would bring! Well, if it would take the hatred from Piscator's eyes, Estrogard would see that he won it. The championship meant nothing to him; he was far more concerned lest a young and gifted dragon should grow old with bitterness. He would do for Piscator what he had refused to do for Max – allow himself to be beaten.

Once more, and for the last time, the fanfare sounded. Once more the crowd was hushed. From a distance it looked as if the two were performing a ritual dance as they moved forward and back, circling warily, waiting for an opportunity to close and grapple. This was not so easy as it might appear. The rules forbade them to use talons or to spit fire. They could wrestle using tails, wings, head and neck, but talons and fire could be lethal and so were not allowed.

The crowd raised a shout – they had closed, and were now rolling and writhing together, their tails entwined, each trying to force the other over onto his back. Piscator opened a wing – then suddenly Estrogard felt pain stab his belly. Under cover of his wing Piscator had clawed his opponent, knowing exactly where to wound. Again he stabbed. Despair flooded Estrogard's mind. This was no game – it had become a fight for life. A third time pain seared his body. Then red anger drove out despair, gave him strength to wrap himself around Piscator's throat and squeeze until his opponent was gasping. Swiftly he released his hold, lowered his head and pushed frantically, furiously . . . Piscator struggled against the force, lashing at Estrogard with his tail, but the blows went unheeded. Estrogard's whole being was intent on pinning down his rival, fire spurted from Piscator's mouth – but too late. Impotently he waved his talons and tail – Estrogard was astride him, the unqualified victor.

The noise about him was thunderous, but Estrogard was unaware of it. Limply he lay on the grass, shaken to the depths by what had happened. The despair returned to him, together with all Max's warnings, and he could not bear to face the crowd. But now the cheering had died away and his name was being called; the silver trumpets rang out again, the drums rolled triumphantly. Blindly Estrogard raised his head to receive the victor's crown. Then he opened his eyes to survey the mob, and flinched at its reaction. A shout rose up from the whole assembly, but it was not all the sound of acclaim. One complete side of the arena rang with hisses and yells of fury; fire and smoke belched from the hostile dragons until a black pall hung over one side, and rapidly drifted until the whole assembly was overshadowed.

Estrogard's supporters, at first mad with triumph, swiftly changed their mood to anger as the smoke choked them. Unbelieving, Estrogard stared in anguish. There was going to be a riot; there would be bloodshed and nothing he could say or do would have any effect except to madden them more.

This, then, was what success meant.

And then, incredibly, thunder crashed in the sky, and without warning torrents of rain broke over the assembly, flooding the arena within seconds. Shocked and gasping, the dragons recoiled, bewildered. Rain like this was new to many of them who spent their winters in caves, and they forgot everything except the need to reach shelter. Sizzling, slithering, they jostled each other in the difficult ascent up the slopes now gushing with natural streams and flooded by the artificial ones which had burst their banks.

Only Estrogard remained, a small red blur in the centre of the deserted arena. His body ached from the wounds, and he knew it was foolish to remain lying there; but it seemed to him that, for once, the water was his only friend amidst so many enemies, and he let it stream over his body. His head drooped. The golden crown floated away on a little gully.

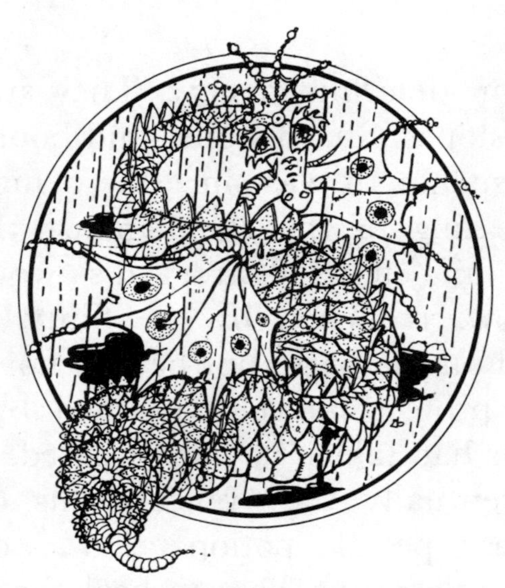

# Rain on Sorrow

"Come on, old man. You'll have to move and get some treatment for those cuts." Max, for the first time in his life was letting himself get wet. Awkwardly he had slopped across the water-logged arena to where Estrogard lay.

"How do you know I'm wounded?" Estrogard's voice was dull as he raised heavy eyes to his friend.

"I'm not blind – or stupid. Come on now."

Slowly Estrogard gathered himself up and stood for a moment. He had no energy, no will to do anything. His body sagged again.

"Estrogard, pull yourself together. If you don't take shelter now and treat those wounds, how are you ever going to get home?"

"I'm sorry, Max. You're quite right." Again Estrogard drew himself up and began to move, with difficulty, but determined now. They struggled on foot up the slopes. Sharp stones and boulders lay in their path, such as it was since the deluge; and the constant beating of the rain against them made every step an effort. Estrogard's wounds were bleeding now, reopened by the flinty rocks they encountered on the path, but he had not the will to fly and so protect himself. Stunned by the turn which events had taken, he hardly cared.

When eventually they reached his cave, Max prepared a special potion that would send Estrogard to sleep and help to heal the wounds at the same time. While it was brewing he wiped away the blood and examined the cuts. He gasped and gave a low whistle – if Piscator had stabbed a fraction higher he would have pierced Estrogard's heart! He said nothing of this to Estrogard; simply bandaged the wounds with soft, sweet-smelling leaves, kindled a warm fire, gave him the potion and left quietly.

Slowly the numbness eased away from Estrogard's mind and he looked around him. He saw the potion and sighed. Max had been good – very good. He wondered why he should have bothered; he had not done any more for Max than for any of the others – and much less than for some. It must be just because Max was such a good fellow.

"Get healed and then home." Something like that Max had said. He drank the potion slowly. Home! It was so long since he had left; so long since there had been any message. All through the games he had brushed aside the loneliness and spent his spare time going amongst the dragons trying to show them that it was not a necessary part of a dragon's life to cultivate violence and nurse secret hostilities. What a waste of time it had been! How they must have been sneering at him, as all the time they stored up in their hearts jealousy and hatred – and hatred of him, Estrogard! Again his head swam and his brain felt numb.

With an effort he dragged his mind back to the present, only to be tortured by new fears. He could not escape the fact that, since the first evening there had been no message. He had turned all possible reasons over and over in his mind as every day he looked for the dove, and every night he went to bed disappointed. Up to now, the reasons had, if not convinced him, at least helped him to accept the homesickness that he always felt away from the mountain and from Paul.

But now it was no use pretending. The dove could have been back and forth several times and she had not reappeared even once. What had happened to Paul? Had some dreadful accident befallen him? Human beings had such short lives. Oh, but it would be too cruel if he were to lose his friend just at this moment when he needed him most.

And if he were not dead – then what other explanation could there be? Out of all that he had considered only one possibility remained – Paul did not want to send back the dove; he had ceased to care.

Sadly Estrogard began to get used to the thought, and the more he considered it, the more likely it became. Had he not just experienced a total rejection by all the dragons? He had thought they accepted – he had even been so foolish to believe that some of them liked him. He had not expected to find genuine friends among them – these, he knew, were exceptionally rare and precious treasures; had it not taken him centuries to find Paul?

He groaned a little. Paul. Oh, it was perfectly understandable. He was away for six months of the year – it was probably hard for the boy to keep remembering him. Then there was such a difference between them – a dragon and a human being – anyone could have told him it wouldn't work.

But it had worked! Up to now, the difference had only made their friendship more exciting; each had shared what he had of life with the other; there had been no difficulties. There was much they had in common – their love of birds and rabbits, of rain and stars, of music and laughter, of light and darkness. They did not spend all their time in each other's company, but that did not matter. It was unnecessary: they were quite content with whatever fun and laughter and happiness they had together; it lasted from one time to the next. Estrogard had believed that, if necessary, it would have lasted forever, for their mutal fire burned brightly and seemed an immortal gift.

Maybe he had been wrong. Maybe he had expected too much from a little boy. Maybe the little boy who had grown up had found someone else to take the dragon's place. Very likely.

"Tell Estrogard that a spark of our fire has kindled another flame." Oh yes . . . that must be it.

The rain outside beat on, and on.

# The Lord of Light

There was, of course, no question of a celebration being held the next day. Even though the rain had stopped during the night, it would take a few days for the sun to dry out the whole terrain. Estrogard stayed confined to his cave, somewhat feverish, and Max toddled up and down between his own cave and Estrogard's, keeping an eye on the patient but leaving him alone when he felt that he wanted to be undisturbed.

Many of the dragons were very busy baling out the arena, emptying the muddy water into the sea. With luck, the grass might be dry enough by the following day to begin the next stage of business – discussions on the place of the dragons in the modern world.

Unfortunately, there were by this stage a good

many dragons who had lost interest in the proceedings. They did not enjoy being crammed on a small island with hundreds of other dragons. They had not taken part in the games; and they had been disgusted by the final part that had proved beyond all doubt that dragons could never, ever live peacefully together. The "place of the dragon in the modern world" did not interest them. They had lived in their various sectors of the world for centuries. Why should they suddenly begin to worry about their place? With these and other arguments they began to drift away, so that the assembly was much smaller when it met the next day.

Max had persuaded Estrogard to come to the meeting. At first he had thought that rest was what he needed, but he noticed that although the physical wounds were healing well, Estrogard was miserable. Thinking that he was depressed because he had found enemies among supposed friends, Max felt that the best policy would be to make Estrogard face the assembly again without delay. He would discover, he hoped, that not all the dragons were against him. Now as he looked around, Max saw with dismay that numbers of those who had left were dragons he had counted on for support. As his eyes scanned the rows, he could find only a few friendly faces scattered amongst the large numbers of enemy ones.

Once again the venerable leaders began with speeches, again the sun was hot; but this time Max was wide awake and it was Estrogard who had difficulty in fixing attention. The chief dragon's voice droned, though occasionally it quavered in a high-pitched treble, for he was old and his voice cracked.

Estrogard gazed up at the sun. He was reminded of the day he had flown across the sea with Paul and nearly been drowned under the sun's beating rays. It had always been sunny when he had been with Paul. Perhaps the dove might come today. She might even have arrived. He turned to look over his shoulder towards his cave. Max nudged him, and he remembered where he was.

". . . and so, for his unfailing care of sunbeams, starshine, rainbows . . ." The speaker's voice held him for an instant, and then his mind wandered again. He saw the rainbow curled around Paul and the stars that danced for joy whenever he came to visit the mountain lair.

". . . we call upon you, Estrogard, to accept the honour of becoming the guardian, the Lord of Light."

There was silence. Estrogard, hearing his name, turned to Max.

"Go on, man. You'll have to go up there onto the platforms" Max whispered.

"What for?"

"Didn't you hear?"

"No, I was miles away."

A murmur had broken out among the crowd. Cheering from a few of Estrogard's friends gathered forces as others, till now enemies, realised that it would be good policy to show enthusiasm for the newly appointed Lord of Light.

Max was briefly explaining to Estrogard what had been said; now the red dragon was making his way slowly through the assembly towards the platform. He shuddered as the crowd cheered, half expecting a repetition of the previous incident. Certainly there were many stony faces turned towards him as he mounted the dais.

The chief dragon made a movement for silence, then his voice rang out as he changed solemnly the words of dedication.

"Estrogard, champion of dragons, friend of the helpless, we here pronounce you Guardian of Starshine, Protector of Sunbeams, Shaper of Rainbows. Your power extends through the whole universe. It is yours to distribute the warmth of the sun and the radiance of the moon, yours to control the phospherescence that plays upon moors and upon the sea. All creatures will depend on your goodwill to give light to their lives. Only the fire of dragons is beyond your control. Rule wisely and generously, according to your nature.

"Estrogard, Lord of Light."

Again the cheers rang out; fire flashed in enthusiasm; there was no black smoke. Estrogard noted this with relief. He also noted, for the first time, how much smaller the assembly was now. Perhaps his worst enemies had gone home. Perhaps, after all, he would address the assembly when the time came, and tell them, as he had all along intended to do, how they could find the key to the kingdom of true happines. The dove might have arrived by now. Even if she had not, he still believed that while Paul had been his friend, true happiness had been his. Despite his present sadness, the message was worth passing on to others. Someone else might find the key and be lucky enough not to lose it.

The noise had died away and the chief asked Estrogard if he wished to address the crowd. But before he could do so, a voice rang out from just below the platform.

"I object!"

Startled, all eyes turned, heads craned, voices murmured and hissed as everyone tried to see who was speaking.

"I object to Estrogard being appointed the Lord of Light. He is unworthy of any high office. Judge for yourselves!" The speaker was Fuhalla.

The murmur was growing louder now; dismayed and angry, the leader called for order.

"Silence! Come up here, Fuhalla. Explain to the assembly what you mean."

Dragons stood aside for Fuhalla who rapidly made his way to the dais and faced Estrogard. Never had such stillness hung over the assembly.

"I accuse you, Estrogard, of having betrayed your nature and every dragon in the universe. You have deliberately taken the form of a human being; you have abandoned your own nature and lived as a man among men."

Consternation broke out among the dragons, but Fuhalla's commanding voice dominated, and forced their attention.

"Moreover, not content with this deception, you have betrayed the secrets known only to dragons to a human boy. You have granted him the power of understanding every living creature. Deny this if you can."

Estrogard was silent. Why should he deny it? There was no crime in what he had done. He tossed his head and drew himself up.

"I will deny nothing. Any right-minded dragon will know that there was no evil, no betrayal in what I have done. Those who accuse me now do so not because they care for their brother dragons, but because they hate me."

"You see!" shrieked Fuhalla triumphantly. "He cannot deny it. Who will now accept such a creature to be the Lord of Light? Traitor!"

The assembly was in a tumult. "Traitor! Traitor!" they yelled, glad at last to have reason for venting their jealous hatred. "Ban him! Kill him! Death to the Traitor!"

Helpless, the dragon elders looked on. It was Estrogard who quietened the mob. Clear and steady his voice rang out.

"Silence!" The riot gradually subsided. All were curious to know what he would say. "You have been waiting – you, Fuhalla, and all those brethren of yours. I had thought to leave this assembly having shared with you a little of the goodness I have met among men and beasts. It had been my hope to show you that the key to the kingdom of true happiness is found in love. But something went wrong. You thought that I was ambitious and you became determined to destroy me. Perhaps you will destroy my body, brother dragons of mine; perhaps you alone, out of all living creatures, are unable to understand the message of love that I have learnt. But never fear, though you may destroy this carcass, the fire within me will never die; it will spread until it has filled the universe . . ."

It was not what they had expected. They were mute with astonishment. Alone, Estrogard rose into the sky, turning his face westwards, and before they realised it, he had winged upwards and away. Then there was confusion, but no one dared follow him. His talk of the key to the kingdom had stirred something deep within many of them, and they began to wonder whether perhaps they had been merely used by Fuhalla as tools of his jealousy.

There was one dragon who had understood Estrogard's message. Max, awakened from his lifelong sleep, believed Estrogard had passed on to him the key. He would seek him out and tell him.

# Part Three

# Perhaps Tomorrow

There was no point in waiting any longer. A wispy moon was already standing in the sky. The sun still had a long way to sink, but he would never come as late as this. With a sigh Paul turned away from the forest; faint strains of fiddles and accordions floated up as he took the path back to the village. May Day revels. How late Estrogard was! He was usually back with the daffodils, but now all the cherry trees were in full bloom; the hawthorns were even beginning to blossom, and still no sign of him.

It had been a long, long winter. The dove – the useless bird – had stayed away for ages and had only returned a week before, with such a garbled message that she might as well not have bothered. Oh – it was not really her fault. As far as Paul could make out from her distracted words, she had left

Estrogard in a very befuddled state after drinking some special dragon brew. This must have upset her sense of direction, for she seemed to have flown round the world the opposite way, and lost her bearings completely. By the time she reached Paul she was gibbering feverishly and talking nonsense.

He quickened his steps as he approached the village, for he was to play the lead fiddle in some of the dances, and the others were already tuning up. He tried to push the thought of Estrogard out of his mind – perhaps tomorrow Mr. Nogard would be there on the mountain path; perhaps he would come in the morning fresh with the dew; perhaps the nightingale would once more waken him; perhaps . . . perhaps . . .

He collected his fiddle, spruced himself up and joined the rest of the band in the village hall.

Out in the forest an owl hooted, a squirrel, disturbed by the rapid footfall, scampered up a beech. From the shadows of the trees emerged a man in a black coat.

# Skippy

Skippy squeezed herself between the crowds jammed around the edge of the hall, trying not to get her skirt crushed or her hair tossed as she wormed her way through. Once in sight of the band she tried to catch Paul's eye, but he was playing a very fast tune and concentrating hard. She tapped her foot impatiently, but it was no good – he'd never look round while he was playing. She picked up a chocolate wrapper from the floor, borrowed a stub of pencil from Old Barney sitting near her, and scribbled a note. The minute the music stopped she passed the note through to Paul. He looked up sharply when he had read it, a puzzled question in his eyes.

"Come outside!" Skippy's lips framed the words though she made no sound.

"After this dance," Paul replied, equally soundlessly.

It was easier to move while the dancing has stopped and, without being noticed, Skippy slipped through the people and went outside. Old Barney, who had observed the whole transaction, smiled quietly to himself.

Impatiently she listened to the sounds as the second dance whirled the boys and girls, the mums and dads around the floor. The hall shook with the pounding and stamping on the wooden boards, while above this the fiddles wailed and the accordions wheezed. Usually a dance was over far too soon, but this one seemed interminable. At last the fiddles twanged to a halt, and after several minutes, Paul emerged hot and breathless.

"I've seen him! He's back," she whispered.

"But you couldn't have, I was waiting up there all the evening. It was sunset when I came away and there was no sign of him."

"I tell you I have seen him. He spoke to me. And he gave me this." She fingered a pendant that hung around her neck. In the light that come from the hall Paul looked at it – a silver medallion with an inlaid design in garnet and gold – a minature dragon.

"What time did you see him?"

"Just a short while ago. I came straight down to tell you."

"What did he say?"

"He asked how everyone was , and then he said

'Do you know where Paul is?' And I said 'Yes, he's at the May revels. I'll be seeing him in a minute; do you want me to tell him anything?' Then he asked me why I was up there by myself, and I said 'Looking for flowers to wear,' and he drew this out of his pocket and fastened it round my neck and told me to have a lovely time at the revels. Then he turned round and walked back into the forest and I ran straight down to tell you."

"I'm going after him."

"Paul, it's dark now. You can't."

"How did he look?"

"He looked a little bit old – he was walking slowly. I thought he looked a bit sad, too."

"I will go. There's only one more dance for me to play in. I'll play that and then I'll go. And if you breathe a word of where I am I'll never speak to you again."

"But the forest, Paul, and the mountain! How will you climb it in the dark? Wait till morning. You've waited all winter. Another night won't make much difference."

"Stop fussing like a grown-up, Skippy. You don't understand."

She tossed her head and pouted. "If it hadn't been for me you wouldn't have known he was there and then it would have been all the same."

"Sorry, Skips. Look, I can trust you, can't I?"

She would not answer, but Paul continued, "When I've played my last dance, will you take my fiddle home with you and look after it for the night and tell Bill I'm sleeping out? They won't worry; I often do that."

"Paul, the forest's dangerous."

"It's not dangerous. Skippy, don't worry – there's nothing to fear in the forest if you keep straight ahead and know where you're going. Mr. Nogard taught me that. Now, promise you won't tell?"

"Promise," she said, a little reluctantly. He gave her hand an affectionate squeeze and they went back into the hall.

# Dark Journey

It was a little eerie going through the forest, despite Paul's bravado in front of Skippy. He could never be quite sure that a tree was just a tree – in this forest they all seemed to have personalities and he would not have been surprised if they had all come to life and moved around to make him lose his way. However, they stayed where they were until he was through, contenting themselves with now and again tapping him on the head and whispering "silly boy" as he hurried through.

Once on the slopes he was amazed to find how bright the moon shone, and to see the sky thick with stars. He could not remember ever having seen so many – you would have thought that all the stars in the universe had been gathered and placed in the little patch of sky that hung over his valley.

It was easy climbing as far as the Dragon Rock, for he knew the route well; from here upwards it became far more difficult. For one thing, it was hard to find a foothold; for another, he had never climbed this section of the mountain – they had always flown from here to Estrogard's lair. Many times he made a false step, mistaking a shadow for a foothold, and slid down again several feet. Near the summit the slope became almost sheer, and he clung on, gripping with his fingernails, knees, toes, worming his way upwards, pushing, pulling, crawling. Sweat stung his eyes; his feet were bleeding – he had taken off his good shoes and left them at the edge of the forest. Whenever the summit came in view, he strained his eyes for any sign of Estrogard. He might not even be there! If he wasn't . . . ! Paul gritted his teeth and struggled on.

By the time he gained the summit, the moon had moved considerably; Paul judged that he must have been a couple of hours on the way. No sign of Estrogard, but he could see, a few paces below him, the quartz slab. His heart was pounding with hope and fear and dread; his throat ached and his knees sagged, but he made the last few steps and sank down upon the gleaming stone.

"Estrogard!" He meant it to be a shout, but it came out as a whisper. He banged with his fists on the slab, hoping to come upon the secret spring which would open it. All Estrogard needed to do was gently to press with one talon – why couldn't he do the same? He felt all over it – no effect.

Voice of the trees floated back to him. "Silly boy ... of course it won't open ... sitting on a mountain calling for a dragon ... there's no dragon ... it was all a dream ... you're not a child any more ... calling for Estrogard. Estrogard won't come back."

"But Skippy saw him!"

"Skippy saw an old man – nothing much in that."

He blocked his ears and rocked back and forth on his heels. He wouldn't believe it! Estrogard was real; he was real and he was a friend. He would come back.

But even with his ears blocked he could still hear the hissing, mocking voices.

"Estrogard!" he murmured. "Estrogard, Estrogard."

There was a stir in the grass at his feet; in the moonlight Paul could see a drowsy rabbit sit up, rub his eyes and peer round. At the sight of Paul he took fright and darted away but stopped after a few yards and scampered quickly back and stared.

"Lor' bless us if it isn't Mr. Paul, sir. Pardon me scarpering like that, sir, but we rabbits can't be too careful on a moonlit night, and we not expecting to find old friends come a – visiting – which, if I may be so bold as to remark, is a bit unusual, in the middle of the night, like."

"Oh, Mr. Rabbit ..." Paul began, but his voice was choked with relief at seeing someone from the old days who still recognised him.

"Well, Mr. Paul, you're right welcome back, and

no matter what time of day or night, a friend's a friend, say I," and he patted Paul's arm with his paw. He could see he was upset.

"And you've come to see your friend, of course," he went on tactfully. "Just back today, and looking very weary, I might add but then you know all about it, I suppose."

"I don't know anything," said Paul rather thickly, because he had such a lump in his throat. "And I want to see him but I can't get in!"

"Ah," said the rabbit, shaking his head. "Nobody can get into a dragon's lair unless he opens it from the inside."

"Then, what am I to do?" Paul's voice was dangerously shaky; he was feeling desperate. Again the rabbit patted his arm.

"Have you knocked?."

"I've banged and banged, but nothing happened."

"No – but have you knocked? You don't need to bang – he won't hear a bang from inside. But haven't you got a special sort of friendly sort of a knock?" He'll hear a knock like that."

Paul thought for a minute, then smiled; the rabbit smiled back.

And then, very gently, he knocked, with a special sort of a friendly sort of a knock.

# Light and Laughter

With his head resting on a rainbow curled into a cushion, and the little sunbeam nestling beside him, Estrogard was asleep. The once golden crest was now sadly copper-coloured, and the red scales were fading into grey. He had done his work well, distributing light all over the world, and had lavished starlight above his own beloved mountain and village. Now he was home at last – not finding Paul he had come straight back to be greeted and welcomed and consoled by his own rainbow and sunbeam, who soon lulled him into a deep, much needed slumber.

Now, in the dark stillness of the deep mountain cave, there came a sound – a thrilling sound, like birdsong and laughter and star-music, but clear and distinct – one single sound, happy beyond all description. The little sunbeam shivered with pleasure; the rainbow trembled, and Estrogard raised his head. Such a feeling touched his heart! Such warmth of joy! Still the sound continued, it floated through the dragon's palace, awakening all the starshine. Crazily the star began to dance and swoop, the sunbeam was spinning ecstatically, the rainbow arched and coiled and wound in and out. The palace was ringing with music, flooded with light. And Estrogard gleamed true gold once more, and his scales were brilliant red. Laughing he stood erect and opened the entrance to his cave.

Moonlight smiled at sunlight; stars greeted stars. Paul came in to Estrogard.

"Just as well I decided to camp out tonight," said the rabbit to himself, smiling in satisfaction. Then, because it was so unusually warm, he put his head between his paws there and then and went to sleep.

There was so much excitement in the mountain palace that it was a long time before Paul and Estrogard could say anything. A few moonbeams had sneaked in with Paul and they were having the time of their lives playing with the sunbeam and the others. They could not understand the reason for so much joy but they joined in the festivities all the same while the dragon and the boy sat back and laughed for sheer happiness.

The rainbow brought a crystal bowl of dew to bathe Paul's sore feet and hands and knees and the sunbeam stroked his cuts and bruises and healed them with her sweet warmth. And at last they all decided they had danced enough so they settled down quietly; but they did not go to sleep for the two friends must have radiant light all the time – that was understood by everyone.

"It's been a long winter," said Paul.

"Very long," agreed Estrogard, wincing slightly as he remembered.

"What happened to the dove?"

"The dove! She only got back last week. Dead drunk – that's what happened to her. She flew round the world the wrong way back and completely lost her memory."

"Oh dear," said Estrogard, "that was my fault. I gave her a celebration drink and sent her off before she had time to recover."

"Well," laughed Paul, "you'll know the next time."

Estrogard sat very still for a moment, then said, "There won't be a next time."

Paul stared at him, hardly daring to hope. "Do you mean you're going to stay with us all the year?"

"I'm not sure. All I know for certain is the I shall never return to visit the other dragons."

Then quietly, without any drama, Estrogard told Paul everything that had happened since he had left him. Sometimes he made him laugh, especially when he described his first encounter with Wilhella and his sleepy friend, Max. But as the story moved on there was no laughter, and when he ended, Paul was very serious.

"They hate you because of me, then – because

you took me to be your friend and shared your dragon secrets with me."

"No, Paul; that was only an excuse – a mean excuse. They hate me just because they hate me. However, they needn't be afraid of my troubling them. I shall not go near them again."

"But how can you avoid it, it you're the Lord of Light?"

"I'll find a way."

"Estrogard, you're not safe here any more."

"Safe?" He laughed reassuringly. "I couldn't be more safe. Here in my mountain cave no one can enter unless I open from within. Besides, those dragons won't follow – they would have overtaken me long since if they had been going to attack. No – there's nothing to fear."

"But you won't be able to come down into the village any more."

"I shall do exactly as I have always done; what would be the point of staying imprisoned in my lair? I might as well be dead."

He was so emphatic on that point and so apparently confident, that Paul felt better and began to chatter about all the things that he had done during the winter, and how he had discovered that Skippy liked doing the same things that he did, and that he didn't need to give long explanations to her because she seemed to understand straight away. He said he had shared a little of Mr. Nogard's secret with her, but not the great secret about Mr. Nogard being Estrogard because he wanted to be quite sure that Estrogard wouldn't mind.

"Do you think she'd really understand?" asked the dragon.

"Yes, I think so."

"Then tell her. And bring her up with you the next time."

By now it was nearly dawn. Estrogard and Paul went out onto the mountain together, to watch the sun rise and to hear the morning sounds.

"I suppose I'll have to go back," Paul said at length.

"Couldn't you stay?" There was a curious pleading in the dragon's eyes that had never been there before.

"Well . . ." Paul saw the look and made up his mind. "Yes, I could. But I'll have to send a message. I'll stay a week."

"A week! That would be very good. It would give us time for everything."

Paul looked at Estrogard quizzically, but the dragon's eyes were full of sunlight reflected from the dawn sky.

"Write a note; the rabbit will take it for you."

"Oh, he'd be all day getting there, poor little fellow, and he'd never get back."

"True, true. Well, we'll find a reliable bird – the nightingale; she knows the way to your home."

"She ought to – she's sung by my window often enough."

So Paul wrote a note to his mother, saying that he was staying out for a few nights with Mr.

Nogard, and she wasn't to worry. He wrote a little note for Skippy, too. "I've met him, and he wants you to come and see him one day. I'll be back soon and we'll go together."

"Good," said the dragon, "I'm looking forward to that."

# Danger

It was a week of wonders. Paul and Estrogard had never laughed so much, visited so many places, seen so many sunsets and sunrises, played with so many stars, as they did that week. Towards the end of the week they called once more on their old friends, the gryphon and the unicorn. This was by now an annual event and the eagle was there too. Paul always loved the visit, though sometimes he became a little bored when the gryphon would begin "Do you remember", and go over all the details of their first meeting. This time, however, there was very little of that. Estrogard had been recounting his troubles with his fellow dragons, and everyone looked grave – too grave, thought Paul, if Estrogard's words could be believed. He had assured him there was nothing to fear. And yet, as they said "goodbye" at the end of the day, Paul had a little cold feeling in his heart. It felt to him as if they were saying goodbye for the last time. There was no fuss: everyone was just extra kind, extra gentle, and the smiles were extra bright.

As they neared home and the mountain came into view Paul noticed a dark patch on the slope, just outside the lair.

"What's that?" he asked, feeling uneasy, though he did not know why.

"Looks to me like a visitor." Estrogard, too, was slightly disturbed, until, drawing close to his home, he recognised the midnight blue and silver coiled, sleeping shape of – Max.

"Max!" he called joyfully.

"Is he a friend?"

"Oh, yes! He's the one who nursed me and gave me back my courage when . . ." he paused. He was about to say "When I thought I had lost the key to the kingdom of happiness", but then he remembered that he had not told Paul this part of the story.

They landed, and again Estrogard called, "Max! Max!" and shook him gently. The sleeping dragon opened a drowsy eye, blinked, smiled and said. "I'm glad I found you."

The quartz slab swung open and the three slid down the opal chute into the palace, where the sunbeam was hiding behind a pillar, ready to pounce on Estrogard; but when she saw the stranger she was suddenly covered with embarrassment and hid inside Paul's coat, blushing and throbbing.

Estrogard welcomed his friend from the East and introduced Paul, called out to the rainbow and the stars who bowed respectfully and lay down as a carpet for Max to glide over. Then they made soft star-music while the two dragons talked of what had brought the blue dragon such a long distance and how he had managed to find the way. After a little while Paul left the two and went to prepare a meal; dragon food took little preparation and was melt-in-the-mouth when it was done. He would have been very quick but for the sunbeam. She had recovered from her shyness once out of Max's presence and made up for her previous quietness by getting into everything Paul touched, and spinning round the rainbow juice as he poured it into a silver pitcher.

While he was gone Max was urgently explaining to Estrogard the latest developments.

"Soon after you left, most of the dragons went home. They abandoned Fuhalla, realising what he was up to. But a few stayed with him . . ."

"How many?"

"About ten. They were planning to follow you. It was hard to overhear their plans because they were suspicious of me, but as far as I could learn, they are coming. It may be one evening after sunset. You'll be all right if you're in your cave – but if you're out or down the valley as a man, you're done for."

"And the boy? Did you hear anything about

him?"

"No – but it would go hard for him if they found him here."

"How long do you reckon they'll take to get here?"

"I was very quick – birds were kind, so were beasts, they told me the way."

"They'll direct the others too."

"Not necessarily – I looked like a friend – the others don't."

That was a point. Estrogard shuddered, remembering the cold gleam in Piscator's eye. The birds and beasts would certainly recognise enemies but they could not hold them off forever.

"You'd have at least another week, anyway."

"And then?" He was not expecting an answer. His brain was working feverishly. Stay in the cave forever? What kind of a life would that be? Stay in the village as Mr. Nogard forever . . . ? Here he paused. That might be a solution. It might be. He would only have a short life then, for human beings died soon, but he would be near his friend, and with the people he had grown to love. It was a possibility. Oh, but Fuhalla was wily. Soon he would discover the ruse, and then Paul, for whom he had given up his dragon nature, would be in danger too.

"I'm prepared to fight them with you."

As Max quietly said these words Paul returned with a much livelier sunbeam than when he had left, and with a splendid meal. He stopped short as he heard Max.

"Fight who?"

Max looked apologetically at Estrogard. He had not meant Paul to hear, but Estrogard said,

"It's all right Max. Paul must hear everything for it concerns him closely. Now we must work together."

"What is it?" Paul was already guessing what Estrogard would say.

"Just that we have come at last to the point where we stand three friends against ten enemies,"

"Three against ten!"

"Friends against enemies. However many they have, friends are far stronger then enemies."

Paul's spirit stirred, determined to stand by Estrogard.

"I'll fight beside you till I die!"

"There'll be no fighting."

Paul and Max both looked at Estrogard surprised, then awed. He was a prince, his eyes glinting with suppressed fire as he tossed his golden crest, fully in command.

Softly he spoke, "We have no need to fight."

"But . . . but . . ." Paul stammered.

"What would you want to fight for?"

"To save your life."

"You said just now," Max interrupted, not understanding, "that we were stronger then they. If they come and we don't put up a fight they'll just kill you . . . then where will you be?"

"All they want is my life, and they think they can take that by slaughtering me. They don't realise that the most important part of me, my fire, can't be harmed."

"A dragon's fire can be put out."

"Yes, indeed it can; if it has only stayed with the dragon and the dragon's body is killed, then the fire will die because it has no home to go to."

"Estrogard's fire won't be put out, Max; it has lived too long with mine. I shall keep it burning."

The two dragons stared at the boy. He seemed to have grown taller, fairer, with the sunlight shining in his face and a star resting on his brow.

"I thought I would be sad to think of losing my Estrogard; I often wondered how it would be when I walked up the mountain path knowing that Mr. Nogard would never come again. Sometimes I have cried a little in the night, imagining how lonely my life would be. I see now that it was a childish way of looking at things. As long as I live, the beauty of Estrogard and the warmth of his fire will stay with me, and wherever I go, people will share the happiness of knowing him. So in people's hearts he will be still the Lord of Light."

It was Paul who now looked like a prince; it was Paul making all the decisions. Max was to go out every day and pass round the word to all the birds and beasts, and even the trees and plants – no one was to tell any dragon where Estrogard lived, but they were to send any enquirers off on a false trail. This would keep them at bay, and it was hoped, frustrate them so much that eventually they would give up the search. Estrogard, meanwhile, would go down into the village just as he pleased, so long as he was back inside the mountain by sunset. That would be no hardship. Life could go on as it always had gone on; they would all make the most of it. . . .

Half amazed but deeply thrilled, Estrogard smiled at Paul.

"I should have known," he said exultantly, "I should have known you'd understand. There is nobody like you. There are no words to describe you. And because there were no words for either of them, Paul put his arms round the dragon's neck and hugged him.

# An Invitation

The plan was working well. Every day birds came to report dragons had been sighted in various places, but they were being scattered North, South and East. The messengers were optimistic – they thought the dragons would soon go home.

Paul and Estrogard were cheerful, but deep down, both felt that it was only a matter of time. They carried on with life as usual. Paul went back home, Mr. Nogard came to the village every day to entertain a new generation of children and talk to those of the old crowd who still enjoyed his company. Summer wore on; roses bloomed, faded, fell and were replaced by new buds. When he could, Paul went back at night to be with Estrogard and find out what was likely to happen. Max faithfully did his work, and at last it seemed as if the danger had passed over.

"When are you bringing Skippy to see me?" asked Estrogard one warm evening.

"Do you still want her to come?"

"Of course. It's very important that she should come and see me in my home. After all she had shared our fire."

"What about tomorrow?"

"Yes – as early as possible."

So when Paul was back in the village that night he called round to Skippy's house.

"Oh, I don't know if she's in," said her father.

"She is – I saw her through the kitchen curtains as I came along."

"Well er – well, come in, anyway."

"I'd rather wait outside, if you don't mind." Paul knew what it would be like inside – mother, grandmother, a few brothers and sisters; he could hardly explain about Estrogard in front of them all.

He waited a long time, but she came eventually, slowly, humming carelessly.

"Oh Skippy – there you are!"

"Well – you took your time, didn't you? I suppose you didn't realise I took your fiddle back home for you two months ago."

"Oh, don't be cross, Skippy. I've something very important to tell you. Mr. Nogard . . ."

"Ugh!" she said, stamping her little foot.

"What?"

"I said ugh! ugh! ugh! ugh!"

"Why?"

"Mr. Nogard, Mr. Nogard. That's all you think of. I hate him."

"But he wants you to go and spend the day on the mountain with him! He's never asked anyone else before. Won't you come? Please! You'd love it!" She said nothing. "And he did give you that lovely pendant – remember?"

Still she said nothing, but looked at the pendant, and Paul could see that she was weakening.

"All right," she said at last, and then they laughed together.

"But you must come with me."

"Of course – and there's something special to tell you about him. He gave you a pendant with a miniature of a red and gold dragon – yes?"

"Yes." He held her hand and said, very gently.

"That's because when he's on the mountain, above the forest, he himself becomes a red and golden dragon."

"Oh . . ." her voice faltered. "I see . . ." She was silent for a long time; her eyes held a faraway look. Things were slipping into place; questions she had asked herself about Paul and how he understood so much were being answered; questions about Mr. Nogard, too . . . she was beginning to see . . . to know . . .

"When will we go?"

"Tomorrow at sunrise."

"I'll be there."

# The Sharing of the Fire

She was there all right. They ran together, and the sea lay still like a burnished mirror, reflecting the many-coloured mountains. When they turned up through the village, past the fields, dew stood like jewels on each blade of grass. Mr. Nogard was on the path waiting; he held out his hands to them, and each took his hand and the three ran through the forest, not once feeling tired or even out of breath.

Once more they paused at the Dragon Rock. Skippy looked at Paul but he motioned her to watch Mr. Nogard. For a moment he had a doubt – would she be able to see Estrogard, or would he remain for her only Mr. Nogard? He need not have worried. Quietly Skippy left Paul's side, and very, very gently stroked the dragon's beautiful crest and shining scales.

"Thank you for letting me see you," she whispered.

Then Paul lifted her onto Estrogard's back, climbed on himself behind, and they soared up to the mountain cave.

It was a day of unparalleled celebration. Old friends from the mountain were there – mice, squirrels, Mr. and Mrs. Rabbit and some of their family, birds who had flown with Paul and Estrogard on their many journeys, the nightingale . . . It was all light and music and happiness. Max now looked young and handsome, and told jokes all day. No one mentioned the danger.

At first Skippy moved as in a dream, but soon she felt at home, playing happily with the animals, for though she did not understand their speech, there was no mistaking their desire to become friends with her. The palace was vibrant with joy.

Only the little sunbeam was different, she would not leave Estrogard, but clung to him all day. And Paul, too, stayed by his side.

Together they moved through the palace, seeing that all the guests were enjoying themselves. Skippy watched them and thought: "That's Paul, all right. It's really Paul, but somehow he's more than Paul."

"I know what you're thinking" – the lovely midnight blue and silver dragon was by her elbow.

"I was thinking that when you look at Paul you think of Estrogard,"

"And when you look at Estrogard you think of

Paul."

Skippy nodded. "And they're both so – so glorious."

"That's because they share the same fire."

She was a little puzzled. "Max, what does that mean?"

"It means that they can never die – each will live on in the other."

She looked at them again, smiled, and suddenly, full of life, ran through the palace, chasing a moon beam.

It had to come to an end. The birds flew out through the vault, affectionately taking leave of Paul and Estrogard. Then Max collected all the small creatures on his wings, carried them out onto the mountain and flew them to their various homes. He would be gone some time, so they closed the vault again.

"Now it's time for us to go, I suppose," Paul sighed a little.

"Just a short while more. We can afford it."

Skippy's laughter could be heard ringing through the halls as she played with stars and the rainbow.

"You're lucky to have found Skippy," said Estrogard. "She will understand everything in time." Contentedly Paul smiled.

Then Estrogard stiffened – Paul sat up. "Tap, tap, tap" – urgently, someone was knocking.

"That's not Max," said the dragon, "but it's a friend. You can't hear any other knocks down here."

Quickly he opened the slab; the eagle fluttered hastily down and the entrance was closed once more.

"Estrogard, Paul, friends, bad news. The dragons are on their way. Some treacherous fool of a bird directed them; they're savage by now – destroying everything in sight."

"How far are they?"

"A couple of leagues to the West."

"Time enough to get down to the village and back. Come, Paul, find your friend."

Paul wanted to stay.

"No, Paul, don't argue now. Remember."

He remembered, yet he still did not want to abandon his dragon. But moments might mean the difference between life and death for Estrogard. He called Skippy.

"Find me!" she cried.

Fool! She thought he was playing. Desperately he raced through the palace, calling her name. "Skippy! Skippy! Come now – quickly!" Still she did not appear. He was frantic. "Skippy, you *must* come!" Then he saw her skirt peep out from behind a pillar. Desperately he seized her hand and dragged her back to where Estrogard was waiting.

"Ouch. Don't squeeze so! You're hurting!"

"Too bad."

He threw her onto the dragon's back, clambered on himself, and they rose swiftly. He just had time to glance back at the cave as the vault rumbled shut. It had taken several minutes to find Skippy;

now as he looked towards the West he saw, blotting out the setting sun, a heavy black cloud approaching. They tumbled off at the Dragon Rock, and Paul faced Estrogard.

"Don't come any further. Go back. We'll be safe."

"No Paul. The forest isn't safe tonight. I must come with you."

"I've been through alone before. Nothing will harm us."

"Any other night perhaps – but not tonight. Trust nothing tonight."

Then Mr. Nogard siezed their hands and once more together they ran. They were through the forest. It had been a nightmare run for Paul, but still Skippy didn't seem to realise the urgency of their flight. She thought it was all part of the day's magic.

"Thank you, Mr. Nogard," she cried with shining eyes. "It was a lovely day."

"Goodbye, Skippy," he answered as she flung her arms round his neck then darted off.

"Come on, Paul. Catch me," she called.

But Paul's mind was on his friend. "You must go," he said urgently. "Go back quickly. You'll be safe inside the mountain." Mr. Nogard was not moving.

Paul's voice was shrill. Still he did not move.

"Please Estrogard! Go back, before it's too late! Save yourself!"

"It's all right, Paul," he said at last, gently.

"There's no hurry."

"But while you're standing here, the dragons may be already on our mountain." Mr. Nogard was looking steadily, calmly at him.

"Yes, that's right."

Suddenly Paul understood. There was indeed, no need to hurry. Estrogard was already too late. He looked round him desperately for help.

"Stay with us, then. I'll hide you. You can stay in my den. I can bring you food every day. The dragons need never know where you are. I'll defend you myself. They won't know you are Estrogard."

Sadly Mr. Nogard smiled. "Do you think I could live like that, knowing that every breath I took was at the risk of your life? They would destroy you when they discovered me and that would not take them long to do."

"But they will destroy you now," cried Paul in anguish.

"Paul." Mr. Nogard's voice was soft but steady. "Paul, look at me." He took the boy's trembling hands and held them firmly. It seemed as if dragon fire was glowing in his eyes, and looking at it, Paul felt its warmth and strength. "Do you think they could destroy this? Why, you yourself have fire living in your eyes. We have nothing to fear. I will be there with you, all the time. You will see me in the sunlight, when the sunbeams chase each other across the fields of dew, and in the sunset, when the sky will burn with my fire. You will see me in the rainbow, light smiling through tears; or in the silver moon rays that make the darkness glad. We will meet in the happy smiles of people, when you let our fire shine out from your heart and warm them. And at night I will always be above you, for I shall be your star."

Paul was no longer trembling, but weeping silently.

"I am not leaving you, Paul. They can kill my dragon's body, but nothing can ever put out our fire. Keep it safe and it will lead you back to me."

The words wouldn't come; Paul nodded dumbly, gripped his friends hands tightly, then let him go. Mr. Nogard unwound the sunbeam and placed her on Paul's shoulders.

"Be gentle with Skippy, Paul. It wasn't her fault. It would have happened anyway."

He was gone. There was neither moon nor stars in the sky and the air was heavy and oppressive. Paul groped his way home and stumbled, dazed to his bedroom. It seemed to him that all life must surely come to an end now, in the blackness of the night. Then there was a blinding flash of lightning, and a terrifying peal of thunder. Never had there been such fire in the sky. All the villagers put out their lights and cowered to bed. It was an electric storm – not a drop of rain, just balls of fire flung back and forth across the pitch black sky, and thunder-bolts hurled like boulders, exploding with a din that must surely have split the mountain.

Paul stood looking out, reckless of any danger. He could see the summit from here, and to him all this fire and thunder could mean only one thing: a united attack on his beloved dragon from the rest of his kind.

Gradually the thunder and lightning spent their fury and moved away over the sea, faint flickers and rumblings marking their passage. Then came the rain, torrents flooding the mountain slopes, drenching the forest, filling the streams. Earth and sky wept.

Still Paul stood motionless by his window. The rain passed and all lay hushed in the darkness. At last, the clouds parted slightly and from the East a cold, silvery light awoke and began to grow, spreading over the sky. Dully he gazed at the sunrise, his mind, far, far away. Then, close to his shoulder, sitting on a hawthorn spray, the nightingale began to sing, gently at first, then passionately, until she forced him to pay attention. Paul dragged his tired eyes from the mountain and turned to look at the little brown bird so close to him. She had stopped singing now and was hopping excitedly from one branch to another.

"She wants something," he thought and automatically searched his pockets for a crust or a few crumbs. But she was not interested in them.

"What it it, little bird? Has the storm smashed your nest? Wait, I'll come," and he swung his legs over the windowsill and dropped to the ground. The nightingale fluttered to his shoulder. She was still very agitated.

"What is it then? Show me." Paul stroked her

ruffled feathers, expecting her to fly ahead of him and lead him to whatever had disturbed her, but she only hopped onto his hand and then back to his windowsill.

He turned, following her, stopped in wonderment, then with a leap sprang joyfully into his room. There was no dragon there, no beautiful Estrogard or friendly Mr. Nogard – but fire, flickering, dancing, radiant and lovely in his very own room. The fire of the red and gold dragon had found its home. Paul stretched out his hands and held the fire. He heard Estrogard's voice, "Keep it safe and it will lead you back to me." And as he touched the flames, the world was filled with laughter – the laughter of a man and a boy, and the thrilling melody of a thrush.